HOMILIES ON THE DIVINE LITURGY

Hieromartyr Seraphim Zvezdinsky
Bishop of Dmitrovsky

HOMILIES ON THE DIVINE LITURGY

by Holy Hieromartyr
Seraphim Zvezdinsky

Translated from the Russian
by Fr. Zechariah Lynch

Uncut Mountain Press

HOMILIES ON THE DIVINE LITURGY

© 2024
Uncut Mountain Press

All rights reserved
under International and Pan-American Copyright Conventions.

uncutmountainpress.com

Scriptural quotations are translated directly from the original Russian text.

Library of Congress Cataloging-in-Publication Data
Hieromartyr Seraphim Zvezdinsky, 1883–1937.

Homilies on the Divine Liturgy—1st ed.
Translated by Father Zechariah Lynch.

ISBN: 978-1-63941-036-1

I. Eastern Orthodox Christianity
II. Eastern Orthodox Theology

... the Liturgy is the diamond, that priceless gift from Christ. The Liturgy is the river, strengthening and refreshing, flowing from the side of Christ. The Liturgy is a golden bridge on which only it is possible to come to eternal life. Lovers of the Liturgy—this priceless diamond, this river that brings to life—remember this testament of Christ. Walk upon this golden bridge which will save you from falling into hell.

From *Homily 4*

Bishop Seraphim Zvezdinsky

CONTENTS

HOMILIES 9
   Homily 1: A Great and Magnificent Gift **9**
   Homily 2: The Church of the Old Testament **13**
   Homily 3: The First Divine Liturgy **17**
   Homily 4: The Divine Lamp **20**
   Homily 5: Sts. Basil the Great and John Chrysostom **24**
   Homily 6: The Holy Temple **27**
   Homily 7: The Heavenly Queen **32**
   Homily 8: Proskomedia **34**
   Homily 9: Sacrificed is the Lamb of God **40**
   Homily 10: Blessed is the Kingdom **50**
   Homily 11: The Psalms of David **54**
   Homily 12: The Little Entrance **58**
   Homily 13: The Liturgy of the Faithful **61**
   Homily 14: Let Us Stand Aright, Let Us Stand with Fear **63**
   Homily 15: The Only True Foundation **67**
   Homily 16: *See Sermon 7*
   Homily 17: The Fragrance of Christ **72**
   Homily 18: Let Us Lift Up Our Hearts **76**
   Homily 19: Holy, Holy, Holy, Lord of Sabaoth **83**
   Homily 20: Take, Eat **89**
   Homily 21: The Elevation of the Holy Gifts **94**
   Homily 22: The Consecration of the Holy Gifts **102**

A PRAYER TO THE NEW HIEROMARTYR SERAPHIM 107

THE THEOTOKOS PRAYER RULE 109

BIOGRAPHY OF ST. SERAPHIM (ZVEZDINSKY) 119

Bishop Seraphim Zvezdinsky

HOMILY 1

A Great and Magnificent Gift

Today, as I promised, I will be discoursing with you on the subject of the Divine Liturgy.

Christ says, "*Take, eat; this is My body,*" and further, "*Drink of it all of you, for this is My blood of the New Covenant.*"[1]

The heavens are filled with a multitude of shining stars; they are all simply the sparks of God's vestments. Of them all, the sun is the most beautiful, most radiant, and most bright. A multitude of sweet flowers cover pastures and fields; of them all, the fragrant rose is the finest and most wonderful. A multitude of rivers, brooks, lakes, and streams flow across the face of the earth; yet they all descend and run into the vast, great, and immense ocean. A multitude of splendid bright stones are hidden in the bosom of the earth; there are sapphires, emeralds, rubies, yet the glistening diamond is more wonderful, purer, and brighter than all.

So likewise, the spiritual world has stars, precious stones, and flowers of the spiritual pasture. The Orthodox Church guards a multitude of amazing stars—the hymns

---

1 Matt. 26:26-28

of praise—but they all converge in the sun of our Church, the Divine Liturgy. There are a multitude of marvelous flowers in the pasture of the Church but the most wonderful rose is the Divine Liturgy. The sacred rites are the many magnificent precious stones but brighter than all, the glistening diamond, is the Divine Liturgy. Every spring, every river—our Holy Mysteries—merge into the deepest and holiest mystery of the Divine Liturgy.

In the Church we have the hands of Christ, His mouth, and His eyes, and also His Divine heart. His hands are the sacred rites; the language of Christ's mouth is His Holy Gospel; His eyes are the Holy Mysteries, through which He gazes into our souls; His heart is the Divine Liturgy. Every Church Father speaks of the Divine Liturgy with delight. Blessed Augustine, a Holy Father of the West, exclaims "*Thy wisdom could have created, could have established for humanity, even more spectacular flowers in the fields, and yet Thy love has been shown forth to the greatest degree possible in the Divine Liturgy.*" And this is why, in the Liturgy, Christ gives Himself to the faithful in His Life-creating Body and Blood.

St. John Chrysostom says the Divine Liturgy is a great and magnificent gift. The very angels of God, if it is even possible to express such things in human language, envy us—mankind—to whom it has been granted to partake in the Divine Body and Blood. Myriads of angels flock to the place wherein the Divine Liturgy is served, and with trepidation they stand round about the Holy Altar, covering their faces, while glorifying and praising the exalted mystery accomplished here. In such a manner, the Holy Fathers speak of the Divine Liturgy; in such awe they stood before it.

The ancient Christians comprehended well the blessing given to people in the Mystery of the Eucharist; daily they approached the Holy Chalice, O how pure their lives were! When they would depart on a long journey, they would take to themselves the Holy Mysteries, together with the cross on their chest, as protection. Our forefathers would always begin the day by attending the Liturgy, only after it would they start the works needed for earthly life. This is how people of a Christian mind valued the Divine Liturgy.

Many names are given to the Divine Liturgy. The first - "Pascha," for thus the ancient Christians and Holy Fathers called it. St. John Chrysostom states, "*The person present at the Divine Liturgy is like the beloved confidant of Christ, for the Liturgy is the Mystical Supper and we, tasting of the Holy Mysteries, as it were, lean in on the heart of Christ and hear its pulse.*"[2] The second name is "Supper,"[3] for here is offered to us the Heavenly Bread[4]—the Life-creating Body and Blood of Christ. The third name is "Eucharist."[5] The fourth is "Fellowship," and the Liturgy is thus named because in the Mystery of Communion we enter into the uttermost fellowship with Christ; through this mystery Christ penetrates into all the members of our body. The fifth is "the Meal;" in a similar manner to "Supper," the Liturgy is called "the Meal"[6] because it is the dinner, the feast, to which the Lord calls His slaves through His servants.

We are the slaves. Yet how many among us are there who, upon hearing the invitation of the King, refuse to

---

2   cf. John 13:25

3   "Trapeza"

4   cf. John 6:32ff

5   "Thanksgiving"

6   Russian – *Обедней*. Originally from the Russian word *Обед* (obed), which is a midday meal. *Обедней* is also a more colloquial way to say the "Divine Liturgy" most of all among the common Russian people (of that time). I have chosen to translate it as "meal."

go? Rather, some prefer to go to their merchandise, some to their field, and others do not want to leave the house because "I have married a wife."[7] The servants of the Lord—the archpastors and pastors—give the call, yet their call is not heard; neither is the call of the Church heard— the call of Christ, the voice of Christ—the Holy Gospels. Not only is the call not heeded but some even place obstacles in the way; they laugh, mock, and sneer at those who would come. Such people do not see that they are but beggars and wretches—pathetic, unfortunate, and accursed. They deprive themselves of the divine sun; the priceless diamond they trample underfoot in their delusion.

My dear ones, my God-given flock, love the Divine Liturgy; guard the fragrant rose of Christ and enlighten your souls with the light of the Divine sun. When you fail to attend the Divine Liturgy, count it as if you lost a day of your life. May there not be found in your midst Tolstoyites,[8] Baptists, and Adventists,[9] and the other sectarians and scoffers who deny the Holy Chalice. May your eyes ever behold the Holy Chalice, may your ears ever hear *"Take, eat"* and *"Take, drink."* Ever may you give thanks to the Lord for this most excellent gift, before which angels tremble. *"Praise ye the Name of the Lord; O ye servants, praise the Lord"* (Ps. 134:1).

---

[7] Cf. Matt. 22:1-14; Lk. 14:16-24

[8] Followers of Leo Tolstoy

[9] All of these groups promote/promoted a strong anti-sacramental ideology.

HOMILY 2

The Church of the Old Testament

Today, I will continue my discourse on the Divine Liturgy.

Yesterday, I said, "The angels envy us" since we have such a marvelous gift, such a treasure, such a priceless pearl—the Life-creating Body and Blood of the Savior, of which we commune in the Divine Liturgy.

Today I will show you how the Church of the Old Testament—the Holy Prophets and forefathers of the Old Testament—only anticipated, that is, foresaw from afar, but yet still strove solely for this, the greatest of all gifts. Christ said, *"blessed are your eyes because they see; and blessed are your ears, because they hear"* (Matt. 13:16). He spoke this to His disciples—how blessed then are we who taste of His Body and Blood! Only in foreshadows and only in types did the people of the Old Testament—the prophets and righteous ones—behold this Gift given to us; even so, what awe overcame their souls!

The prophet Moses as he was tending his flock, beheld a bush, a thorn bush, that was burning with fire and yet was not consumed. He desired to draw near but heard a voice saying, "*Moses, take the sandals off your feet, for the place where you stand is holy ground*" (Ex. 3:1-5). The bush, according to the interpretation of the Holy Fathers of the Church, signifies the Most Holy Virgin, who bore God the Word, the divine fire, and He left her incorrupt and most-pure. Yet the bush also signifies the Divine Mysteries, which, like fire, burn our passions and yet do not consume us. Anticipating this mystery, Moses, full of awe inspired delight, removed the sandals from his feet; thereby showing forth an example of the holy fear with which we must approach the Holy Mysteries. Speaking further, Moses says these remarkable words, "In the Tabernacle"—which was the first Temple—"set before Me the bread offerings, set them before Me continually."[10] These bread offerings stood in the Tabernacle for one week,[11] after which time the priests would eat them on the Sabbath. These bread offerings were a prototype of the Holy Mysteries.

Solomon says, "*Wisdom built her house and she supported it with seven pillars. She offered her sacrifices; she mixed her wine in a bowl and prepared a table … 'Come, eat my bread and drink the wine I mixed for you'*" (Prov. 9:1-3,5).[12] Behold, here are repeated the very words that we hear in every Liturgy! Here Solomon speaks of Divine Wisdom, who is Christ. The seven pillars are the seven Mysteries of the Orthodox Church. The supper is the Divine Liturgy, at which is offered the Heavenly Bread and Wine. The archpastors and pastors are servants who must unceasingly call every believer to the Feast. The ringing of the Church bells are also a call to the Supper. The bread and wine spoken of in this proverb are but prototypes of the Bread and Wine, which are

---

10 This seems to be a paraphrasing of the Old Testament commandment given by the Lord to Moses; see Leviticus 24:5-9.

11 From one Sabbath to the next Sabbath

12 Compare also with the words of the Lord Jesus in Matt. 26:26-29; Mk. 14:22-25; Lk. 22:14-20.

offered here in our temple, in a dread and wondrous manner, as truly the Life-creating Body and Blood of Christ. And so, King Solomon could only offer a foreshadowing of the holy mystery of the Divine Liturgy.

The Prophet Isaiah says in the Bible that he beheld a marvelous vision; he saw the Lord sitting on an exalted throne—the throne was surrounded by the six-winged Seraphim, with two they fly, with two they cover their feet, and with two in awe they cover their faces, crying unceasingly, "*Holy, Holy, Holy, Lord of Sabaoth.*" With fearful reverence the prophet cried out, "*Woe is me! I shall die!*"[13] *Because I am a man of unclean lips.*" But the Lord spoke to him, "*Be not afraid!*" A Seraph then flew near and taking tongs, he took a burning coal from the altar of God and touched it to Isaiah's mouth (Cf. Is. 6:1-7). In this vision, the tongs, according to the interpretation of the Fathers, are the hands of the Virgin, which received the Son of God. These very hands are still reaching out to us. The burning coal is the Holy Mysteries, for their flames purge away our lawlessness.

The great treasures that have been given to us were but glimpsed through visions in the Old Testament; with such awe were even the foreshadows treated! Purified of every filth the prophet Malachi ... [break in original text][14] ... "I have loved you," says the Lord.

Such was the anticipation and teaching of the prophets. But we do not even cherish the Holy Mysteries, in our midst are those who do not ever draw near to the Chalice. About such people it is written, "*the Queen of the South will rise up in judgment along with the people of this generation, and she will condemn them, for she came from the ends of the earth to hear the wisdom of Solomon; and behold someone greater than Solomon is*

---

13 In Russian - *Погиб Я!*

14 Bear in mind these homilies were preserved in Samizdat form in Russia.

here" (Lk. 11:31). In such a manner both the Old and New Testaments speak of the gift of the Divine Liturgy.

Father John of Kronstadt says, *"Having been present at the Divine Liturgy, fall on your face and give thanks to the Lord, Who has granted you such an incredible joy. My friends, remember the rule of the Holy Fathers: a person who misses three consecutive Liturgies[15] is to be denied a Christian burial. Do not miss these Suppers of the Lord. Consider that feast day lost in which you failed to be present at the Divine Liturgy."*

I will tell you a parable—one Christian owned three thousand, six hundred, and eleven pounds of bread[16] and traded it all for rags. Tell me, did he act wisely? No. Rather very unwisely. How much more unwise are the actions of a person who trades the Bread of Life for the rags of earthly existence. The Lord Himself calls us to His Mystical Supper, and to Him such answers are given - "I must go to market; I must tend my garden; My field is not yet sown!" Yet, do not such people know, unfortunate ones, that the seed scattered on the earth during the Divine Liturgy will come up sickly, stunted, and will not bring forth fruit?!

My friends, pray with me thus: "Lord, we thank Thee for Thy Gift; we thank Thee that Thou hast granted us to be present and hear the Divine Liturgy and to even taste of Thy Most-Pure Body and Thy Life-creating Blood. We pray Thee also on behalf of those who have departed from Thy Holy Chalice, for those who have no desire to find consolation in Thy saving Mysteries. Do Thou enlighten and draw them to Thyself, that they too would be with us in Thy Holy Church."

---

15 It seems Sunday and feast day Liturgies are implied.

16 The original text uses the old Russian measurement of a pood. One pood equals 36.11 pounds. The original text reads, "owned one hundred poods of bread."

HOMILY 3

The First Divine Liturgy

Today, my friends, I desire to discourse with you regarding the topic of who served the Divine Liturgy for the first time, and where it was served for the first time. In the heavens there is the bright Sun of righteousness—everlasting, not created by anyone, self-illuminating, and ever pouring forth eternal light. This Sun is the Father. From this Sun radiates the most luminous Divine Ray, Who together with the Sun is eternal and beginningless, and the Creator and Sustainer of all things. This Ray is the Son of God. It is this Ray, this Ray of light most glorious, that lit a miraculous lamp on earth. This lamp He has fueled not with oil but with His ever-filling Divine and Pure Blood.

This lamp, my dear ones, is the Divine Liturgy. This lamp has been lit by the very Son of God, the beginningless Ray from the beginningless Sun—the Father. The Son lit this lamp during the last days of His earthly life; it burst into flames for the first time in the upper room of Zion—in the hour of the fulfillment of the Mystical Supper. You see who and where for the first time celebrated the Divine Liturgy.

The Holy Evangelist and Holy Fathers describe the first Liturgy <... >[17] He Who was both sacrifice and minister of this first Liturgy—the Savior—washed the feet of His disciples and sat with them. Further, it says, Christ took bread. No, it was not only bread that He took in His most-pure hands, not bread but you, a sinful soul. It is you He took in His immaculate and most-holy hands. Having taken the bread, He raised His eyes, lifting them to heaven, to the Father. He gave praise to the Father and showed Him the sinful soul He held, as if to say, "I take this soul and purchase it, not with gold or diamonds, for I purchase it with My blood and with the sufferings of the Cross."[18] Further it is said, Christ blessed the bread, and He did so doubtlessly expecting His death on the Cross. He made the sign of the Cross on the bread. Having given thanks, the Lord then broke the bread.

No, it was not bread that He broke, for He crushed His flesh. After this Christ gave the bread to His disciples, proclaiming these words which are repeated every time the Liturgy is served: *"Take, eat"* and *"Drink of it all of you."* Having said these words, Christ the Savior added this gentle loving counsel: *"Do this in remembrance of Me."* This New Covenant established by Christ the Savior has brought great joy to the lives of people. Tasting of the Body and Blood of Christ, people partake of the Divine nature[19] because first and foremost the Lord has entered into the house of their souls. Human souls become the temple of God—O, what eternal and sublime joy this is!

The first followers of Christ did not forget His commandment—*"Do this in remembrance of Me."* And behold,

---

17 Break in original text
18 Cf. 1 Peter 1:18-20
19 Cf. 2 Peter 1:4

for nineteen centuries the bloodless sacrifice has been offered on this earth.

In the flow of nineteen centuries there has not been one day in which the Divine Liturgy was not offered, and it will not cease as long as the world exists, as long as this earth exists.

No type of enemy power is able to extinguish this lamp of the Divine Liturgy which is lit by the very Divine Ray Himself. Satan has stirred up storms, he has raised up the most cruel abuse, and has incited raging waves of suffering—all of this so to extinguish the lamp of the Divine Liturgy! Yet he has not succeeded, nor will he ever succeed.

With the coming of the Antichrist a renewed persecution of the Divine Liturgy will begin; once again it will have to be hidden beneath the earth, as in the time of the first Christians. But even during the time of the Antichrist the Divine Liturgy will be served; even on the last day of the world—when angels shall gather all people to the Judgment Seat, both those living and those raised from the graves—the Divine Liturgy will be served, but it will be served in Heaven on that day.

My dear ones, guard this Divine lamp, love the Divine Liturgy; strive to satiate yourself in this fountain of life. Consider the day lost when you are unable to hear the Liturgy. The Church calls everyone to this feast of God, even those who are home due to need and mothers of families. The Church strives to remind everyone through the ringing of bells towards the singing of "It is Truly Meet" that at that moment the dread Mystery of the Divine Liturgy is being offered.

HOMILY 4

The Divine Lamp

Let us continue our discussion on the Divine Liturgy.

From our temple today, my dear ones, let us travel back to the distant pagan times of Antioch and the first centuries of Christianity. Christians are being persecuted, they are being arrested and locked up in terrible prisons, after which they are led away to the arenas and given over to be devoured by wild beasts; they are smeared with tar and lit on fire, so that they are revealed as living torches.

At this time in Antioch, it happened that persecutors seized the priest Lucian[20] together with his flock. He was condemned, and while in prison his flock said with sorrow to St. Lucian, "Our dear Father, how will we partake of the Holy Mysteries?" Lucian lay motionless on a hard board; his legs were shackled so that he could not stand up. "Do you have bread and wine?" he asked. "Yes, some kind people have brought some," they answered. "Only, how will you serve the Liturgy, for we have no altar?" "Bring here the bread and wine and place them on my chest, let it be a living altar for the Most-Pure Mysteries of the Lord,"

---

20 Feast Day, Oct. 15th

Homily 4: The Divine Lamp

proclaimed the imprisoned priest. And so they brought the bread and wine and St. Lucian served the Divine Liturgy on his own chest. He together with all the assembled Christians partook of the Holy Mysteries.

In such a manner did the early Christians serve the Liturgy! They did not have fixed prayers or rituals. During these times of persecution, they served the Liturgy underground, in the catacombs. In the evening they would start the service and finish as the sun began to rise! They did not finish because they grew tired of prayer but rather because it was dangerous to live as a Christian. In various places of the pagan world the Liturgy was offered, but not in every place every day. For example, in one place it would be offered four times a week, as St. Basil the Great says about his flock. In very early times, Christians gathered together every day but most of all on the day of the Resurrection, which is called the day of sun and bread—in remembrance of Christ's Resurrection it is called "Sun of Righteousness," and it is called bread in remembrance of Holy Communion.

The service would start with readings from the Holy Gospels and the Acts of the Apostles, and then prayers began. They did not say or read prayers from a prayer book but rather from the heart; prayer was fervent and impromptu. Their hearts, warm with the grace of the Holy Spirit, gave forth wondrous hymns and songs. Almost none of these prayers and teachings are preserved; only in fragments from later times do we find indications that some of our prayers in the Liturgy repeat the songs of the early Christians.

And so it is today, our exclamation *"Let us love one another..."* is but cold words. For the early Christians it was full of deep meaning, then they felt, in their underground churches, that they in truth loved one another and that they were very close to each other. As a sign of this love and brotherhood, those present would exchange a kiss, men with men and women with women. The priestly ministers also gave the holy kiss to each other. And so, at this moment of the Liturgy, the sounds of hymns were intertwined with another sound—the holy kiss. This tradition remains today in only a weak form—the priestly ministers kiss each other on the shoulder and the deacon kisses the cross on his stole. In the same way today when we exclaim *"Let us lift up our hearts,"* only the choir coldly responds, *"we lift them up to the Lord."* But it was not so in the time of the early Christians, for they all, with all their heart, proclaimed these words; for they truly abode in the Lord with all their soul. They did not notice the passing of time, nor did they feel tired. Only the dawn, because caution was needed, forced these Christians, who had gathered in the evening, to disperse to their homes. So long did they pray!

This is spoken of in the Acts of the Apostles. The length of their prayer is evident from the account of the miraculous saving from death of the young man who fell out of the window during the sermon of St. Paul.[21] So fervent was the prayer of these Christians that they did not even notice how time passed. Only after long prayer did the Communion of the faithful take place. In ancient times, Christians received Communion daily, both men and women. Later they began to commune less frequently, but no less than once a week. Believers would come up to the altar to receive the Holy Mysteries, since at that point no iconostasis separated the sanctuary from the nave. First the men would commune and then the women. For those too ill or those in official service, the deacon would afterwards bring them Holy Communion at home. So pure were the lives of the early Christians that they were able to be prepared every day to receive Holy Communion.

---

21 Cf. Acts 20:9-11

This is how the Liturgy was in ancient times. If today, someone asks you, my friends, "what is the Divine Liturgy?" answer—"it is the Testament of our Savior." He Himself has said, *"Do this in remembrance of Me."* He has left for us as a testament the service of the Liturgy—to taste of His Life-creating Body and Blood. Answer—the Liturgy is the diamond, that priceless gift from Christ. The Liturgy is the river, strengthening and refreshing, flowing from the side of Christ. The Liturgy is a golden bridge on which only it is possible to come to eternal life. Lovers of the Liturgy—this priceless diamond, this river that brings to life—remember this testament of Christ. Walk upon this golden bridge which will save you from falling into hell. Beloved ones, do not listen to those who run away from the Liturgy and those who flee from the Chalice. These are unfortunate, lost, and pitiable people. They are unable to see the brilliance of the diamond; they are fainting from thirst and have wandered far away from the river of Christ; they fall into the chasm while trying to flee from the bridge. But you, always cry out: *"Blessed is He who comes in the Name of the Lord."*

HOMILY 5

Sts. Basil the Great and John Chrysostom

Today I will only speak a little bit about the Divine Liturgy. The last time, I told you that it is called the Divine lamp, the life-giving river, and the priceless diamond. At first this river was not enclosed with banks and the diamond was unset. The Divine Liturgy did not have established and uniform prayers, nor a set rite.

According to tradition, from apostolic times the Liturgy was called that of St. James, the brother of the Lord, or St. Mark, or St. Peter; yet these were not required rites for everyone. Up into the fourth century the order of liturgical celebration and hymns were set by each bishop for his flock. You are already well acquainted with the strength of soul and the fervor of prayer of the ancient Christians. Their prayers lasted all night and they did not know exhaustion during the time of prayer. Yet, with time such fiery prayer cooled and all-night prayer became burdensome for believers. Some began to be absent from the Liturgy. Condescending to their weakness, St. Basil the Great established a shortened rite of the Liturgy, that is, when compared to the ancient rites. This rite of St. Basil we now celebrate only ten times a year. St. John Chrysostom further reduced the hymns and established an even shorter liturgical rite. The diamond received a precious setting, the river was directed into wonderful and flourishing banks, and the lamp received a bright flame.

The manner in which St. Basil the Great established the rite of the Divine Liturgy is witnessed to by saints Probus and Amphilochius.[22] According to the words of St Amphilochius, St. Basil prepared a very long time for this holy work. He long besought Christ the Savior to reveal His holy will to him and to bless him in the preparation of the liturgical rite. His prayers were heard. The Lord revealed to St. Basil that he may undertake the work. Six days he spent in prayer and fasting and at the end of these prayerful preparations he stood before the Holy Altar and with fervent hymns sang the Liturgy. These hymns and rites were then recorded. From this time the Liturgy has not changed. The Sixth Ecumenical Council decreed that nothing should be added or removed from these prayers that have been established by these two great Fathers of the Church.

Why was it necessary to establish a consistent rite for the Liturgy? So that the lamp would not be extinguished, so that the river would flow on a straight path, and so that the diamond would not be damaged. An established rite was necessary to guard from the introduction of some false and heretical practices into the ceremony of the Liturgy. Even more so, in the fourth century substantial heresy was manifesting in the Christian Church. Therefore, Saints Basil the Great and John Chrysostom directed the river

---

22 Possibly St. Amphilochius of Iconium whose feast is November 23rd

into a safe channel. May they help you, beloved ones, to remember and love the Divine Liturgy, about which Fr. John of Kronstadt, that foremost servant of the Liturgy, testifies, "*Prostrate yourself and give thanks to the Lord Who has granted you to be at the dread and Holy Liturgy.*"

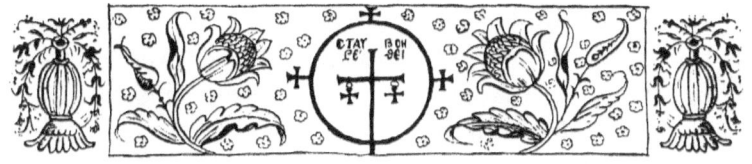

HOMILY 6

The Holy Temple

Today, my friends, I will be speaking to you about the holy temple.

Every temple is built according to a particular plan; even our own church was built according to this ancient plan. A church consists of three sections: the narthex, the central part (the nave), and the altar area (the sanctuary). In ancient times the narthex served as the area of prayer for catechumens (those preparing to receive Holy Baptism) and "the kneelers"[23]—such was the name given to Christians who, due to serious sins, lost the right to stand with all the faithful. They were called "kneelers" because they would kneel before those who entered the church and ask, "please pray for us for we have greatly sinned."

In ancient times the central part (the nave) was not separated from the altar area by a partition, which is called an iconostasis. The iconostasis only appeared in the time of St. Basil the Great. The reason why he built the iconostasis is related in his life. St. Basil received baptism while already

---

23 Or "the fallen." In Russian *Припадающим*

an adult and the holy river Jordan served as the font for him, the place where our Lord Jesus Christ was baptized. Before St. Basil was baptized, lightning flashed forth and from it a dove flew out and descended to the water, stirring it. In remembrance of this miracle, an artisan fashioned a silver dove which was hung over the altar where St. Basil served as a hierarch. He always prayed fervently and because of this the Lord always worked a miracle for him—at the moment of the offering of the Holy Gifts at the Divine Liturgy, the dove's wings would flutter as if alive. Once as St. Basil prayed the words *"And make this bread ..."* he noticed that the dove remained motionless. Confused, the saint fell on his knees and begged God to reveal to him the source of disfavor. In those times, deacons stood by the altar to shoo off insects, of which there are many in the southern regions. St. Basil noticed that one of the deacons was staring out into the nave; he was gazing on the face of a pretty girl. Kindled with zeal for the glory of God, the fervent Basil drove the deacon off and removed him from the service, after which the Lord once again manifested the miracle. From that time St. Basil introduced the iconostasis so that servers of the altar would not be distracted during the time of prayer. At first the iconostasis was a light curtain, and then it became a small partition, and eventually over time became what we have today.

The worshipping faithful gather in the central part of the temple, the nave. In the sanctuary two holy things are found: the altar table[24] and the table of oblation. The altar table is placed in the sanctuary with special and sacred rites. During the consecration, it is carefully washed several times and then it is covered in the *katasarkion*[25] - a pure white linen cloth that is fastened in a crosswise manner

---

24 The Russian word *Престол* may also be translated in English as "throne."

25 Also *Srachitsa*. In Russian *Срачица*

with a cord. After this the altar is covered with a bright cover, typically brocade, and then the other holy articles are placed on it.

Everything I have outlined has a deep meaning. According to the interpretation of the Holy Fathers, the three part structure of the temple reflects, on the one hand, the Divine Trinity, and on the other hand, the narthex represents the earth, the nave the visible heaven, and the sanctuary the heaven of heavens. The altar table represents the throne of God. Throughout the Holy Church we are reminded of the Holy Triune-God; everywhere the Lord manifests Himself as the Consubstantial Trinity.

Our souls also speak to us of this. Our mind witnesses to the Divine Mind, Who created the world—God the Father. Our heart witnesses to Divine Love—the Son of God, Who is Consubstantial with the Father. Our will is in the image of the Divine Will—God the Holy Spirit.

If we contemplate the coverings of the Holy Altar table, then even here we find many images. The altar table is washed so that it shall be a place for the presence of the Lord. A person is also washed in water at baptism and according to the testimony of the Holy Apostles is a temple of God. The white altar covering reminds us of the baptismal garment, and the crosswise tying of the cord speaks of the cross that is received at baptism. The bright covering speaks of the radiant glory of God that even the flaming Seraphim, who are before the Throne of God, are unable to endure; with two wings they cover their faces and with two they cover their feet so as not to be scorched (by the glory). Therefore, with what awe should we come before the throne of God?

The nave represents the visible heaven and we the faithful must be like the stars in the sky, illumining our souls with prayer.

The relics of martyrs are set in the altar table in remembrance of how the first Christians prayed in the catacombs; moreover for them, at times, the very graves of the martyrs served as altar tables. The Holy Altar table should be consecrated by a bishop, but now, when a bishop is not always able to travel to the consecration of a temple, he at least consecrates the *antimension*. *Antimension* by translation means "instead of the table." The *antimension* is made from a rectangular piece of cloth, either silk or fine linen, and a piece of a holy relic is sewed onto it. On the cloth is depicted an icon of the preparation of our Lord's body for burial, together with the four evangelists. Upon it is also an inscription indicating the place to which the *antimension* was given and the bishop who gave it. The *antimension* is kept folded inside another special cloth covering on the altar table. During the Divine Liturgy it is unfolded and upon it are placed the Holy *Diskos* and Chalice. It is not possible to serve the Divine Liturgy without an *antimension*; with it one may serve the Liturgy even in an ordinary room, even in a tent, and on a simple table instead of the altar table. Besides the *antimension*, a Holy Gospel book, a cross, and a tabernacle containing the reserve Holy Gifts, are placed on the altar table as well. Thus, on the altar table is present not only the invisible but also the visible presence of the Lord, which is manifest in the Holy Gospel and Holy Gifts.

The table of oblation stands to the left of the altar table and the service of the *proskomedia* is served on it. In ancient times the bread that was brought by the faithful for the service of the Lord's Supper was placed on it.

This is but a short outline of the temple, in which we gather for the divine services. Every aspect and everything in it speaks to us of the presence of God. With what reverence then must we stand here before the throne of God? Before it the angels stand with awe and we are likened to them as we sing hymns of glorification in the temple.

How pitiful, how unfortunate are those people who do not love the temple of God; those who exchange the glory of God for the rags of this world; those who because of worldly cares are robbed of the desire to be in church.

My friends, love the temple for it is the place of God's continual presence. Hurry and come to church, most of all on feast days. Strive to be likened to the angels who unceasingly sing God's praises.

HOMILY 7

The Heavenly Queen

The priest, before beginning the Divine Liturgy, vests and washes his hands while praying these words from Psalm 25: "*I will wash my hands in innocency.*" What does this mean? If understood in a literal manner, then the priest together with everyone present, most of all those preparing to receive Holy Communion, must be clean as clear crystal—so pure and innocent that their deeds are purified by this innocence, otherwise how could one approach the offered Sacrifice? But is this even possible? Who of us is able to say of himself that he is this pure? Who is free of sin? Who is so pure of thought that he has the boldness to read these words? If they are understood in a literal manner, then the priest first of all people—and after him everyone else—must run out of the church! Yet, the Holy Church knows our weaknesses, and thus she comforts us with this explanation: the words "*I wash my hands in innocency*" speak of the purity of the Heavenly Queen. The bowl and instruments for washing represent the Mother of God, in whose purity the priest, the communicants, and everyone present are purified. Just one drop from the

Homily 7: The Heavenly Queen

Heavenly Queen is all that is needed to wash clean our deeds. Therefore, before the Liturgy it is good to pray to the Mother of God that she would grant us even the littlest drop of her purity. On the evening before receiving the Holy Mysteries, it is a profitable practice to fulfill the rule of praying *"Theotokos and Virgin, rejoice..."* one hundred and fifty times (the Theotokos Rule).

HOMILY 8

Proskomedia

The Lord says, "I am the bread which came down from heaven" (Jn. 6:41). The bread is His Divine Body and His Pure Blood—Holy Communion, which ever strengthens, enlivens, and purifies us. Holy Communion is the Sun of righteousness ever sanctifying our life. From this Sun shines forth three rays; It is the diamond set in the ark of three sections.[26] The Divine Liturgy consists of three parts. From ancient times the Service has been subdivided in such a manner because even the first liturgy in the upper room of Zion consisted of three parts.

At the Mystical Supper was first of all the preparation. The Lord told His disciples, *"Go and prepare the upper room"* (cf. Lk. 22:8). After the preparation the Lord sat at the table with His disciples (but Judas did not remain until the end of the supper, he "departed," as the catechumens depart, not having baptism). Finally, [...][27] the Lord began the sacred rite and under the forms of bread and wine, He gave the disciples to taste of His Body and Blood. And so,

---

26 A reference to the ark of Noah, cf. Genesis 6:16
27 Break in original text

Homily 8: *Proskomedia*

the Divine Liturgy consists of three parts. The first part is the *proskomedia*, which is a Greek word because the whole Divine Liturgy came to us[28] from the Greeks. *Proskomedia* means "offering."

The bread for Communion must be made from wheat and it must be leavened. The shape of the loaf must be round and made of two parts. Round wheat bread is taken in memory of that bread which the Savior used when completing the first Liturgy. The round shape reminds us of a *denarius* coin and indicates that we have been bought by Christ the Savior Who gave Himself for us; He Himself has purchased us. The bread is called the *prosphora*, that is, an offering. It is called by this name in remembrance of the faithful who would bring bread to the church for the service of the Holy Liturgy, much as we today bring candles, oil, and other such things (in offering). The two parts of the *prosphora* speak of the two natures of Christ—human and divine. For it is by this *denarius* that we have been purchased, such is the sacrifice that the God-Man voluntarily offered on our behalf, Himself being the Son of God and the Son of the Virgin. At the Liturgy, five *prosphora* loaves are used.[29] "Why is this?" you may ask me. Simply look at the Cross—five loaves are offered in memory of the five wounds of our Lord Jesus Christ.

Now I will move on to an explanation of the Liturgy itself. I have already told you that it is composed of three parts, the first of which is called the *proskomedia*. It is dedicated to the commemoration of the Nativity of Christ. As Christ was born in obscurity and practically unknown until the age of thirty, when He was revealed to the world, so the *proskomedia* is served in the altar (sanctuary) with the holy doors closed. The sufferings of Christ are also com-

---

28 I.e., the Russians

29 This is standard Slavic practice. Greek practices uses one loaf.

memorated in the service of the *proskomedia*, but as if in anticipation [...][30] in a manner such as the Righteous Simeon the God-bearer foresaw them.

Before offering the Liturgy, the priest acknowledges his weakness and sinfulness, and feeling holy awe before the great service into which he is entering, he turns to the Lord in prayer seeking help. This is why before approaching the Holy Supper he stands before the [holy doors of] the iconostasis in fear; confessing his helplessness, he strengthens himself in prayer to the Lord. The priest has already been preparing himself for service since the past evening[31]; now having entered the temple he must, above all else, be at peace with everyone in his mind and forgive everyone every offense. People often speak of unworthy priests, and some folks announce that because of such priests they do not come to church and do not respect clergy because some behave in an unworthy manner. O, what thoughtlessness and what religious ignorance! Are the accomplishing hands that hold forth the changed mysteries in the Chalice those of an angel or an unworthy priest?

The Lord said, "*The scribes and Pharisees have seated themselves in the chair of Moses. Therefore, whatever they tell you to observe, observe and do, but do not imitate their works*" (Matt. 23:2-3). The Lord spoke these words about priests who were sinful, depraved, and embittered to the core. St. John Chrysostom says a person should be thankful to God that Holy Communion is given to him by a weak priest because if the Liturgy were offered by an angel of God, he would not allow sinners to approach the holy things.

Acknowledging his weakness with fear, the priest calls upon the Lord for help. Before the holy doors the priest prays, "*O Heavenly King*" through the "*Our Father.*" In recognition of his sinfulness he prays, "*Have mercy on us, O*

---

30 Break in original text

31 Through his prayer rule of preparation for Holy Communion

Lord, have mercy on us...." Here he, as a priest, asks that his iniquities be forgiven according to the limitless mercy of the compassionate God, and he then proclaims, "*We are His people.*" Further, he beseeches the Most-Pure Virgin to "*open the doors of compassion*" because she is "*the salvation of the Christian race.*"[32]

Having said these prayers, the priest then bows to the image of the Savior that is next to the holy doors and kisses it as he prays, "*Thy Most-Pure image...*" and he then also bows to the image of the Mother of God and kisses it while praying, "*Make us worthy of mercy, O Theotokos, fountain of tenderness ...*" He then proceeds to kiss all the other [primary] icons on the iconostasis while chanting their *troparia*. The veneration of the holy icons is offered to supplicate the aid of the Mother of God and the holy God-pleasers on behalf of the weak and sinful priest before the offering of the dread Liturgy. On the other hand, by this veneration the priest also witnesses that our Orthodox Church fulfills the decrees of the Seventh Ecumenical to honor holy icons.

Then the priest stands before the royal doors with his head bowed and prays, "*O Lord, stretch forth Thy hand....*" Again he begs for grace-filled help and still he refrains from entering into the service of the Liturgy. Yet again he asks for strength to complete the service of the Liturgy, so that standing uncondemned before the awesome throne he may offer the bloodless sacrifice. This prayer, as it were, strengthens him and he finally resolves to enter the altar. Yet before entering the altar, he turns and asks for prayer and forgiveness from the gathered faithful, seeking support from them in his weakness.

---

[32] All quoted texts are excerpts from prayers used during the priestly entrance prayers. The full prayers may be found in most Liturgy service books.

With the words of the psalm in his mouth, "*I will enter Thy house...*"[33] he enters into the altar. He makes three bows before the Holy Table and kisses the Gospel and cross which lay upon it, as if the Lord Himself is sitting on His throne of glory. The priest then makes three bows towards the east and proceeds to vest. Vestments represent that the priest must lay aside everything earthly and be clothed in the grace of God. As the priest vests himself in the sticharion, he prays, "*My soul shall rejoice in the Lord, for He hath clothed me with the robe of gladness; as a bridegroom He hath set a crown on me; and as a bride adorns herself with jewels, so hath He adorned me.*"[34] Then with the appropriate prayers, he vests himself in the remaining vestments. All of these prayers call upon and exalt the strengthening power of God's grace. When fully vested, the priest then washes his hands while praying, "*I will wash my hands in innocence ....*"[35] It should be said that in ancient times all the faithful washed their hands upon entering the church and for this purpose a washstand stood at the entrance. St. John Chrysostom says the faithful washed their hands two times, once upon entering the church and the other when they exited as they gave alms. I myself remember, when I was a boy, before entering an old temple that our family attended, we washed our hands in a bowl according to this ancient custom.

Fully vested, the priest then approaches the table of oblation and a final time turns to God with prayer before starting the *proskomedia*, bringing to remembrance the Redeeming Sacrifice of Christ. Offering three bows, he reads, "*God cleanse me a sinner and have mercy on me,*" and "*By Thy precious blood Thou hast redeemed us from the curse of the law ....*" The priest then proclaims the blessing, "*Blessed is our

---

33 Psalm 5

34 Cf. Isaiah 61:10

35 Psalm 25:6-10

God, always now and ever and unto the ages of ages," and thus he begins to offer the *proskomedia*.

I will say more about this at another time but right now I want to remind you again, my friends, to love this diamond of God—the Divine Liturgy. Be present at the offering of the Liturgy with fear and reverence. Call to mind how I told you even the angels themselves envy[36] that we have been given such an incalculable gift. The angels descend from the heavenly realms to be present at the offering of the Liturgy! The venerable Seraphim[37] witnessed this presence of the angels. The disciples of our venerable father Sergius saw how an angel served with him[38]; other saints have very similar testimonies. How then could we not lay aside everything earthly so to taste of this spring of Life?

---

36 cf. Homily 1
37 St. Seraphim of Sarov
38 38 The disciples were Isaacius the Silent and Macarius. See *The Northern Thebaid, Monastic Saints of the Russian North*, St. Herman of Alaska Brotherhood. Platina, 2004. pg. 35, for the full account in English.

HOMILY 9

Sacrificed is the Lamb of God

My friends, if you are asked, "Who are you?" how would you answer? Answer in this way: a Christian! Yes—Christian—what an honorable name. For this name the first Christians did not spare even their own lives; for this name the martyrs received terrible sufferings, even unto death. What delineates a person with the title of Christian from everything else? [Communion in] the Life-creating Chalice. A Christian, out of all the peoples of the world, is one who receives of the Divine nature of Christ the Savior.[39] A Christian partakes of Communion at the Divine Liturgy—this is why he must treasure the Liturgy beyond measure. I tell you again, count the day as lost in which you were not able to be present at the Divine Service. For it is the Divine lamp, lit by Christ the Savior Himself; it is the diamond purchased with His very Blood.

We have already begun to speak about the *proskomedia*, which is the first part of the Liturgy. The priest, making the exclamation *"Blessed is our God,"* takes the *prosphoron* loaf

---

39 Cf. 2 Peter 1:4

Homily 9: Sacrificed is the Lamb of God

that is prepared to serve as the Lamb in his left hand, and with his right he makes the three-fold sign of the cross over the top of the *prosphoron*.[40] He then pronounces, "*As a sheep led to the slaughter,*" as he cuts along the right side. He then cuts along the left side with these words: "*Or as a blameless lamb before its shears is silent, so He opens not His mouth.*" Then cutting along the upper side, the priest says, "*In His humiliation His judgment is taken away,*" and cutting along the lower side, he pronounces, "*Who shall declare His generation?*"[41]

These four prophetic proclamations all relate to Christ the Savior. He truly was meek and silent before His enemies, as a lamb is before its owner who has the deciding say over its life. The third verse is of special significance; it proclaims Christ the Savior was so humble that He did not demand the application of the law at His judgment. The Sanhedrin condemned Him in only one night, which violated all the laws of judgment, yet the Savior did not protest against this lawlessness. The fourth verse, on the other hand, indicates the unique origin of the humble Lamb, the God-Man, His generation—His origin—cannot be known because it is Divine.

After cutting all four sides, the priest then lays the *prosphoron* on its right side and cutting [the bottom] takes out the holy bread, it now being in a square form,[42] while saying the words, "*For His life was taken up from the earth.*"[43] The priest then turns the *prosphoron*, with the seal facing downwards, and cuts it in cross-wise form[44] while saying, "*Sacrificed is the Lamb of God, Who takes away the sins of the*

---

40 The priest typically repeats "*In remembrance of our Lord and God and Savior Jesus Christ*" with each signing.

41 All four verses are taken from Isaiah 53:7-8 LXX

42 A reminder of the New Jerusalem, cf. Rev. 21:15-16

43 Cf. Isaiah 53:8 LXX; John 12:32

44 Taking care not to cut through the seal. The *prosphoron* loaf bears the seal of the cross with the words, "IC XC NIKA."

world...."⁴⁵ This first piece that is set on the *diskos* is called the Lamb because it represents Jesus Christ. At the time of the Eucharist, it is this piece that becomes the Body of Christ.

The priest then turns the Lamb over, so the seal of the cross is again facing up, and pierces the right side,⁴⁶ saying, "*One of the soldiers pierced His side* ...."⁴⁷ And having pronounced the words "*At once there came out blood and water,*" he pours wine and water into the chalice and blesses it. In this moment, the setting aside of the Lamb also images the Most-Pure Theotokos; according to the interpretation of the Holy Fathers, this portrays the Nativity of Christ and His coming forth from her.

The priest images the Holy Spirit, through Whom the incarnation of the Son of God was accomplished, and the deacon is likened unto the Archangel Gabriel, the herald of the incarnation of Jesus Christ. As the priest places the Lamb on the *diskos*, he images forth the placing of Jesus Christ in the manger—the *diskos* represents the manger and the cave. It also represents, at one and the same time, the new tomb into which Joseph and Nicodemus placed Jesus Christ.

The priest then takes the second *prosphoron* and says, "*In honor and memory of our most blessed Lady Theotokos...*" and removing a [triangular] particle, he places it on the right side of the Lamb⁴⁸ while saying, "*The Queen stood on Thy right side....*"⁴⁹ This particle represents the Most-Pure Virgin Mary, whose prayers the priest calls upon, for the Mother

---

45 Cf. John 1:29; 3:16-17; 6:33, 57

46 All designations of right and left are from the perspective of the Lamb. The Lamb is pierced under the letters IC.

47 Cf. John 19:34-35

48 From the perspective of the Lamb, thus from the priest's perspective it would be his left.

49 Cf. Psalm 44:10, LXX

Homily 9: Sacrificed is the Lamb of God

of God prays unceasingly for the whole world before the throne of God.

The third *prosphoron* is called "of the nine ranks." It is called by this name because nine particles are taken from it in honor of all the holy God-pleasers. According to the teaching of the Church, the heavenly hosts are numbered in nine ranks. In the same manner, the saints—the Church triumphant—are numbered in nine ranks. In honor of these nine ranks, particles are taken from the third *prosphoron*. Special importance is given to this loaf, and thus the priest must diligently pray over it. The saints who are invoked when removing the particles from this third *prosphoron* give unto it, as it were, their grace. For this reason, this *prosphoron* is especially given to the sick and suffering, those who stand in great need of being fortified in spiritual strength.

Taking this loaf, the priest proclaims, "*Of the honorable and glorious Prophet, Forerunner, and Baptist, John*" as he removes the first particle, which will begin the first row.[50] He places it on the left of the Lamb. He then takes a second particle from this first row, saying, "*Of the holy and glorious prophets: Moses and Aaron, Elijah and Elisha, David and Jesse, the Three Holy Youths, Daniel the Prophet, and all the Holy Prophets,*" and places it below the first. This second particle is dedicated to all the Holy Prophets who were heralds of Christ's coming. The third is dedicated to the Holy Apostles [and is placed below the second].

The first particle of the second row is placed in memory of the Holy Hierarchs: first of all are commemorated the great hierarchs, Basil the Great, Gregory the Theologian, and John Chrysostom; then various other Ecumeni-

---

50 The rows move from top to bottom

cal[51] hierarchs together with those of Russia.[52] The priest then removes the second particle of the second row in commemoration of all the Holy Martyrs, both male and female. The third particle of this row (the sixth altogether) is dedicated to the memory of the venerable Fathers and Mothers. This particle completes the second row.

The first particle of the third row is placed in memory of the Holy Unmercenary Healers and Wonder-workers. The eighth particle is placed in honor of the Holy Forebearers of God, Joachim and Anna, who served the cause of salvation by bringing forth the Most-Holy Virgin Mary. While taking this particle, the priest also commemorates the saints of the day and the patron of the temple [in which he serves], together with all the saints. The ninth particle is dedicated to the memory of St. John Chrysostom.[53]

Taking the fourth *prosphoron*, the priest remembers the Patriarch,[54] all Orthodox hierarchs, and the local bishop as he removes a particle and places it at the foot of the Lamb.[55] He then removes particles for the living [faithful],[56] while saying, "*Remember, O Lord,* [and the name]..." and places them next to the first [for the hierarchs]. The fifth *prosphoron* is dedicated to the departed. The priest remembers the

---

51 Universal

52 Here are commemorated hierarchs of significance for certain lands and local churches, which would vary from country to country.

53 Or St. Basil the Great depending on which Liturgy is served

54 Or leading Metropolitan of the local Church is commemorated

55 It is interesting to note that St. Seraphim omits mentioning the particle that is subsequently removed with the words, in current practice, "Remember, O Lord, our land and its Orthodox people." I believe that in Imperial Russia the Tsar was typically commemorated at this point. It is possible that he omits the commemoration of the civil authorities because, it seems, these homilies are given after the Soviets took power.

56 Only Orthodox Christians, both living and departed, may be remembered on the *diskos* during *proskomedia*.

names of the departed while saying, "*Remember, O Lord...*" and removing the particles he places them below those for the living. Last of all the priest removes [from the fourth loaf] a particle for his unworthiness. Thus, the fourth *prosphoron* is dedicated to the remembrance of the living members of the Church and the fifth for the departed. These commemorations at the *proskomedia* have great significance because at the end of the Divine Liturgy the priest places all these particles into the Chalice with the Holy Mysteries, while praying, "*Wash away, O Lord, the sins of all those here remembered, by Thy precious Blood ....*"

The priest asks the Lord to purify and wash away, in His Life-Creating Blood, the sins of every person he has remembered at the *proskomedia*. This is why it is so important for the departed to be remembered during the *proskomedia*. The particles that are removed for them are washed in the Blood of the Redeemer; this mystery lightens any burdensome sin for our departed brethren. If you love your departed relatives, have them commemorated. Maybe sometimes you yourself are unable to request their commemoration, in such a case ask someone else to give their names for commemoration at *proskomedia*. There is no better gift you could offer on behalf of your departed loved ones.

On Mount Athos there exists an ancient custom: after one year the bones of a departed monk are exhumed. If they are clean and white, then they are interred again with honor as the brethren rejoice that their brother was pleasing to God. Clean, white bones are considered an indication that it is well for the soul of the departed. On the other hand, if the exhumed bones are dark, then the monks transfer them to a particular room and pray intensely to the Lord on behalf of the departed one. Only when the bones lighten do the brothers cease their intense prayer for the departed, for this indicates that the Lord has cleansed the departed one of their sins.

Do you see how important commemorations are, do you see how they aid the departed? Do not miss an opportunity to have the departed commemorated and in doing so they also pray for us. Although they cannot help themselves beyond the grave, they are able to help us because they see our lives clearer than we ourselves do and therefore also what is most beneficial. Thus, they especially pray for us when we commemorate them in prayer.

Having completed all the commemorations, the priest takes the thurible [censer] and says, "*Incense we offer Thee, O Christ our God....*" He then takes up the star-cover[57] and places it on the *diskos* while praying, "*A star came and stood over the place where the young Child was.*"[58] At this moment the Nativity of the Savior is remembered, together with the appearance of the wondrous star. The incense represents the presence of the Holy Spirit. The priest and deacon image forth the celestial hosts who with trembling awe looked upon the birth of the Savior of the world. Then the priest, having censed, covers the holy bread and *diskos* with a veil, while saying "*The Lord reigns; He is robed in majesty....*"[59] He then covers the chalice with another veil while saying, "*Thy virtue has covered the heavens....*"[60] In closing, he covers both the *diskos* and the chalice with a large veil, which he censes, while praying, "*Cover us with the shelter of Thy wings....*"[61] These coverings represent, at one and the same time, both the swaddling bands in which the Holy

---

57 In Greek - *Asterisk*; In Slavonic - *Zvezditsa*
58 Cf. Matthew 2:9
59 Cf. Psalm 92 LXX
60 Cf. Habakkuk 3:3
61 61 Cf. Psalm 16:8; 60:5; 90:1-4

God-Child was wrapped at His birth and the burial shroud in which Christ the Savior was wrapped for His burial.

Thus, at the *proskomedia* two of the greatest events are commemorated at one and the same time: the Nativity of Christ and His death on the Cross together with the sufferings He endured. They are celebrated, as it were, in anticipation because in the *proskomedia* the Church speaks to us: "And for what purpose was Christ born? For this purpose, that He would save us by His sufferings." Still, the main focus of the *proskomedia* is the birth of the Savior. Thus, at the moment when the priest censes the covering aer for the *diskos* and chalice he is just as if with the host of angels beholding the birth of the Son of God, and therefore he cries out three times in rapture, "*Blessed is our God, Who art thus well-pleased: Glory to Thee.*" Blessed is our God, Who was so well-pleased that He poured out His mercy on us to the point that He chose to take our human form! In this moment is embodied the amazement of the angels as they stand before the ineffable love of God for mankind. The angels themselves are astounded by the birth of the God-Man.

The priest then reverently bows three times before the table of oblation, as if before the very manger of the God-Child. He then reads the incredibly wondrous prayer of the offering, which Father John of Kronstadt never read without tears of tender compunction, "*O God, Our God, Who didst send the Heavenly Bread, the food for the whole world....*" With this prayer, the priest witnesses to his weakness before God and asks that He still permit him to serve without condemnation the sacred mysteries for the sake of the Son of God and for the blessing and illumination of the people. The priest does not hope on his own strength, for coming to the dread service of the Divine Liturgy he places his hope on the heavenly and strengthening aid of God's grace.

After this the priest concludes the *proskomedia* with a dismissal. Following the dismissal, the priest censes the table of oblation together with the Holy Gifts; he then censes the altar table in cross-wise fashion, saying, "*In the tomb with the body, in Hades with the soul as God....*" Following this, both sacred ministers, confessing their sinfulness, run to the mercy of God asking for forgiveness of their sins. To this end, they recite the 50th Psalm of David[62] with special attention, for it is an icon of repentance.

Then with tender supplications to the Holy Spirit they ask Him to come and purify us from every impurity and human weakness. These supplications are concluded with the hymn of the angels in honor of Christ's Nativity. Thus, having been cleansed of their sins and placing their hope on the mercy of God, the sacred ministers are as though united with the angelic hosts who sing the glorification of the Consubstantial Light Who has come into the world. "*Glory to God in the highest and on earth peace, goodwill towards men,*"[63] cry the heavenly powers with delight and together with them the sacred ministers offer three bows. The ministers are images of the angels. As the celestial ones beheld the birth of the Savior and announced this joy to the people, so the sacred ministers are preparing to announce Him standing present in the temple with the faithful. The priest prays "*Glory to God in the highest...*" with his hands uplifted, which represents the fluttering wings of the angels as they stand bright, astonished, and in wonder before the incarnation of the Son of God. As if seized with the sacred awe of the celestial ones, the priest prays, "*O Lord, open Thou my lips ....*"

The priest then kisses with reverence the Gospel that lays on the altar and the deacon kisses the altar itself; in doing so they greet the King of kings Himself Who sits

---

62 According to the Septuagint (LXX)

63 Cf. Luke 2:14

upon the altar as a throne. The deacon, with head bowed, raises the end of his orarion[64] with three fingers of his right hand and says to the priest, *"It is time for the Lord to act, bless master."* To this the priest responds, *"Blessed is our God, always, now and ever, and unto ages of ages."* And the deacon asks him, *"Pray for me, master;"* the priest answers, *"May the Lord direct thy steps."* *"Remember me, holy master,"* the deacon asks yet again. *"May the Lord God remember thee in His Kingdom, always, now and ever, and unto ages of ages,"* the priests responds.

This dialogue between the priest and deacon has deep meaning, according to the interpretation of the Holy Fathers, it represents the assembly of the heavenly powers who in unison announced to mankind the joyous tidings of Christ's Nativity. The angels beheld this great wonder with fear and holy awe, and in such a manner announced this wonder to the people in holy dread. Therefore, with great awe the priest and deacon approach the proclamation of this message, seeing how they are but men who are weak and sinful and even less worthy [than the angels] to speak of Christ's Nativity. For this reason the deacon so ardently asks the priest to pray for him because it falls to him to be the first in announcing the great tidings to the people. Having read the angelic glorification, the priest and the deacon through it also call upon the angels to help them. Behold, what a feeling of holy awe must be filling the soul of the sacred ministers and the faithful who are present at the completion of the *proskomedia*. This fellowship with the heavenly powers completes the *proskomedia* and the Liturgy commences. In ancient times, when the sanctuary was open, this dialogue took place in the midst of the temple [in the nave], as it is preserved in the hierarchical Liturgy.

---

64 Deacon's stole

HOMILY 10

Blessed is the Kingdom

The second part of the Divine Liturgy bears the name of "The Liturgy of the Catechumens." It is named thus because catechumens—those preparing to receive Holy Baptism—are permitted to be present while it is served. Besides catechumens, Jews and pagans [unbelievers] could be present at this portion also, if they desired to hear the service. In ancient times this whole section of the Liturgy took place in the middle of the church [the nave]. In those days there were not yet set prayers because from the mouths of the faithful worshippers sprang forth fiery hymns and brief prayerful sighs, from which later our [current] songs and litanies were composed.

The deacon, having prepared himself for the joyful proclamation of Christ's Nativity, exits the altar [into the nave] through the north door and comes before the holy doors.[65] Here he makes three bows while praying quietly, "*O Lord, open my lips...*" after which he lifts his orarion in his

---

65 Typically Orthodox churches are built with the altar facing east. Thus, on the iconostasis the north door is the door to the left of the holy doors.

Homily 10: Blessed is the Kingdom

right hand—like an angel's wing because he represents an angel in that moment—and proclaims with a loud voice, *"Master, bless!"* The priest answers from the altar, *"Blessed is the Kingdom of the Father, and the Son, and the Holy Spirit, now and ever, and unto the ages of ages!"* To this the people respond, *"Amen!"* Amen, which means you have spoken truly and rightly. Before this exclamation, the priest takes up in his hands the Holy Gospel and with it makes the sign of the cross over the Holy Altar. This action has deep significance, the Holy Gospel is a symbol of our Lord Jesus Christ Himself. The Cross is the instrument of our salvation. In making the sign of the cross with the Gospel, the priest is proclaiming that our Lord Jesus Christ, by the way of the Cross and His sufferings, has saved us; He has opened up to us the blessing of the Kingdom, which is commemorated in this priestly exclamation.

Behold the profound meaning here! The priest commemorates the sufferings of the Savior on the Cross, Whose birth the sacred ministers had only just determined to proclaim. The priest proclaims the Kingdom of the Son of God, in the name of the Trinity, *"Blessed is the Kingdom...."* At the very start of the Divine Liturgy the Kingdom is proclaimed. It is not an earthly kingdom nor is it a kingdom established through force and oppression. No, a Kingdom of peace is proclaimed, *"Blessed is the Kingdom of the Father, and the Son, and the Holy Spirit!"* An earthly kingdom is a passing kingdom but the Kingdom that the priest proclaims will abide unto the ages of ages. It is this Kingdom that the angels proclaimed to the world when they sang, *"Glory to God in the highest...."* At this point in the Liturgy the sacred ministers represent the angels, and the deacon stands before the people as the angels stood before the shepherds.

The tidings of Christ's birth brought joy to all the world, and the early Christians responded with fervent hymns to the priest's exclamation announcing the advent of the blessed Kingdom. For us today, the great litany follows the exclamation. In ancient times it was not said at this point in the Liturgy; this is why there is no priestly prayer that accompanies this litany as is the usual custom. Rather at this point, in ancient times jubilant songs poured forth [from the faithful]. After the great litany the antiphons are sung, which means "responding voices." These hymns are named thus because they are sung alternately between two choirs, as if calling one to the other. Currently, the antiphons are often sung in a very shortened form and by only one choir. This is very incorrect and in ancient times it was not this way. We need to revive the ancient practice of singing the antiphons antiphonally.[66]

In singing the antiphons we call to remembrance the prophets and forefathers of Christ the Savior.[67] During the first part of the Liturgy[68] the angels flocked to worship the birth of Christ; now the prophets are hastening to worship Him. Now thundering Elijah and Elisha enter into the temple, together with the fiery Isaiah! These Old Testament evangelists and proclaimers of Emmanuel so clearly depicted His sufferings, it is as if they beheld the sufferings of Christ with their own eyes. And with them enters the king, poet, and prophet David the Psalmist, and with him also the wise Solomon, to glorify Christ. David, especially, spoke many times about Christ—His birth, sufferings, and death he described with remarkable exactness and clarity. It seems as if everything took place before the very eyes of the prophet, even though he lived many years before the appearance of the Savior.

---

66 Alternately between two choirs

67 In current Slavic practice, the antiphons are portions of Psalms 102 (103), 145 (146), and the Beatitudes.

68 I.e., The *Proskomedia*. See previous homilies

Each antiphon is accompanied by a quiet priestly prayer. The little litany is said at the end of the first and second antiphons, which starts with the words, *"Again and again in peace let us pray to the Lord."* The Kingdom of peace that the angels announced is being called into the midst of our human existence. *"Help us, save us, have mercy on us, and keep us, O God, by Thy grace."* Four expressions of grace are supplicated here. We ourselves can do nothing without grace, and here we make our appeal to the very fountain of Grace—God—seeking His grace-filled help. *"Help us"* means to encompass and cover us with His protective grace.

All around is temptation; all around is the intrigue of the enemy. I am perishing! Encompass me, help me, save me—this is our entreaty! Like Peter cried in the midst of the stormy waves, *"Save me for I am perishing,"*[69] so we beg not only for protection and covering but also to be saved, if we have already begun to sink in the storms of misfortune. Save us, snatch us, extricate us from the abyss of calamity. *"Have mercy,"* this is the third type of help. If we were unable to hide ourselves behind the shield of Thy help, if we did not hold fast in the midst of the storms of temptation, and did not take hold of Thy hand, but rather fell into temptations—please forgive us, have mercy on us, and be compassionate to us in our infirmities. But today we have such little grace-filled help in the moment of temptation—no, from henceforth keep us because only beneath Thy protection are we able to commend ourselves, each other, and everyone and all our life to Thee. This is the very tender meaning of these petitions.

---

69 Cf. Matthew 14:30.

HOMILY 11

The Psalms of David

On this day when we commemorate the fiery servant of the altar, St. Mitrophan, I will continue with my explanation of the Divine Liturgy. Together, my friends, we will examine the inspired psalms of David, which are marvelous in their depth of thought and the strength of their prophecy. During the Divine Liturgy, you sing certain psalms which are called antiphons. I have already told you that antiphons are the songs of the prophets who have come to bow before the birth of Him Who delivered them from the darkness of hell.

The first psalm (Ps. 102)[70] of the king and prophetic-singer David starts with exclamations of delight and wonder, "*Bless the Lord, O my soul.*" Behold, O my soul, what a joyful miracle stands before you: the very Lord Himself has come to save you, therefore bless Him! As we move on in our singing, this delight is only strengthened, for not only do we sing "*Bless the Lord, O my soul*" but also, "*All that is within me bless His Holy Name*"—with my inner strength,

---

70 According to the numbering of the Septuagint (LXX)

with all of it, bless the Lord! What a magnificent prophecy! Right now, are we not blessing the Lord and His Holy Name with all the strength of our life which has been renewed in Christ?

Of what name does the prophet speak? Of that which the Lord Himself has proclaimed, that name which the whole world pronounces with trepidation—Jesus the Savior. This is the Name that David foresaw. *"Bless the Lord... and forget not all that He hath done for thee."* Do not forget His gifts because they are infinitely great. By His power He has cleansed you from all your iniquities. Are we not cleansed by the blood of Jesus Christ from all the sins that torment us? He heals your every disease and illness; further the psalmist foresaw how He would deliver you from this corrupt existence. He is risen and we are risen; He crowned you with His mercy and compassion, and He fulfills your good desires. Renewed, your strength[71] shall rise like an eagle.

The prophet further exclaims, *"The Lord is compassionate and merciful, longsuffering and of great kindness"* (vs. 8). What overflowing mercy! The Lord is not wroth to the end, even though we may deserve it. Moreover, He does not deal with you as you deserve, nor according to your iniquities. He has not given unto you, He has not dealt with you, as your sins deserve. No, rather, His mercy is eternally great; He has spread His mercy over you like the great expanse between heaven and earth. Not only has He covered you with His mercy, He has *"removed our iniquities from us, as far as the east is from the west,"* that is, completely removed them. *"Like as a father hath compassion upon his sons, so hath the Lord had compassion on those that fear Him"* (vs. 13). Yet again the prophet prophetically says, *"He knoweth whereof we are made"* (vs. 14). Through the incarnation He has known us, His creation; He has remembered that we

---

71 Or youth

are but earth and that a person's days are as grass and as a flower of the field—so short is his earthly path. *"The Lord in heaven hath prepared His throne"* (vs. 19), says King David, and he foresees that everyone will bless the Name of God. *"Bless the Lord, all ye His angels, mighty in strength..."* (vs. 20). And with even greater strength, he calls *"Bless the Lord, all ye His hosts,"* (vs. 21) together with all His works; with holy delight he ends, *"In every place of His dominion, bless the Lord, O my soul"* (vs. 22).

The whole of this psalm is permeated with thankfulness before the generous compassion of the Lord and with holy delight before His majesty. The second antiphon expresses even more of the prophet-king's delight. He does not simply call his soul to bless but he praises and pours forth his delight, and he does so in such a manner that, it may be said, he himself embodies praise, for it is said of him that he "danced and played" before the Ark.[72]

"Praise the Lord, O my soul," he proclaims and answering himself, says, *"I will praise the Lord in all my life, I will chant unto my God for as long as I have my being"* (Ps. 145:1). Do not put any hope in people, for in them there is no salvation. Their spirit will depart and leave them and they will return unto the earth. But whoever has the God of Israel as a helper, such a person is blessed; God is the Creator of all things and He will give judgment and protect the wronged. All those who sorrow will find protection in Him; He gives food to the hungry and He looses the fettered and gives freedom to the prisoners; the blind He enlightens with wisdom and He lifts up and protects the proselytes, orphans, and widows. The psalmist finishes his psalm with joyful solemnity, *"The Lord shall be king unto eternity ... unto generation and generation"* (Ps. 104:10).

While the antiphons are being sung, the priest says certain prayers that, it may be said, summarize all the themes

---

72 Cf. 1 Sam./ 1 King. 6:14ff

Homily 11: The Psalms of David

that are sung in the antiphons. *"O Lord, our God, Thy power is incomparable. Thy glory is incomprehensible."*[73] Here, as in Psalm 102, is glorified the infinite mercy and inexpressible love for mankind of God, and His tender mercies are invoked upon those gathered in prayer. The second (priestly) prayer calls the blessing of God upon His Church and inheritance. The second antiphon ends with the hymn that was composed by Emperor Justinian the Great, *"Only Begotten Son."* The angels glorify Him, the prophets praise Him, and now with the words of Emperor Justinian the race of humanity glorifies Him and cries, *"Save, O Lord, save us!"*

---

73 From the first priestly prayer of the Antiphons

HOMILY 12

The Little Entrance

The earthly life of our Lord Jesus Christ up until the point of His being revealed to the people, that is, His life lived in obscurity in Nazareth, is represented in the portion of the Liturgy from the singing of *"Only Begotten"* through to the little entrance. The little entrance represents the Savior's baptism and the beginning of His preaching [ministry]. In the hymn composed by Justinian the Great, Emperor of Byzantium, we remember the worship offered by the shepherds, and together with them the whole human race, to the Lord Jesus Christ at His Nativity. Preceding His manifestation to the people, the commandments of blessedness are sung; above all else, they depict for us the image of the Lord Jesus Christ Himself, His likeness during His earthly life. At the same time, these commandments indicate to us how a person must receive the Savior's teachings and what spiritual qualities the followers of Jesus Christ must possess.

At the little entrance a candle is carried [in procession] and it is followed by the Gospel and the priest.[74] The candle

---

74 If a deacon is serving, during the little entrance the deacon carries the Gospel and the priest follows after.

signifies the Forerunner of the Lord, John; the Gospel—the Lord Himself. The deacon who carries the Gospel exclaims, *"Let us pray to the Lord."*[75] Then the deacon,[76] while standing in front of the holy doors, elevates the Gospel for the glory for the Holy Trinity Who was revealed at the baptism of the Lord Jesus Christ; he then exclaims, *"Wisdom, stand upright,"* and makes the sign of the cross with the Gospel. In this moment, the Baptism of the Lord is commemorated. The word "wisdom" reminds us that this mystery—the mystery of Theophany—is inaccessible to us through our human reason. The words "stand upright" are prescribed so to call all the weak, lazy, and incontinent ones standing there to attention and reverence towards the service of the Liturgy.

Following the little entrance, the *troparia* and *kontakia* of the feast [of the day] are sung. In this moment, we are with our prayer appealing to the Lord who revealed Himself to the world and we call upon the saints as intercessors for us. Then the "Thrice Holy" hymn is sung—the song of the angelic powers before the Throne of God. With this hymn we glorify the Holy Trinity. The Holy Church elucidates the origin of this hymn in this manner: at one time in Constantinople there was a terrible earthquake and the people were terrified by this fearful misfortune. In the midst of the earthquake [during a procession], a young child was lifted up into the heights and then descended back to the earth. The young child told the crowd gathered around him that while lifted up in the heights, he heard a song sung by the angels, *"Holy God, Holy Mighty, Holy Immortal,"* and to this the people added *"have mercy on us."* When this prayerful hymn was sung, the earthquake ceased. In this manner, the

---

75 This is commonly said between the deacon and priest as they are making the entrance, after the exclamation the priest quietly says the prayer of the entrance.

76 Or priest, if no deacon is serving

"Thrice Holy" hymn also entered into the Divine Liturgy and other church services.

After the singing of the "Thrice Holy" comes the reading from the [Epistles of the] Apostles, which is the remembrance of the preaching of the Lord's disciples. The reading of the Gospel is the preaching of Jesus Christ Himself.

HOMILY 13

The Liturgy of the Faithful

After the reading of the Gospel and when the litany of the catechumens finishes, the liturgy of the faithful begins. This portion of the liturgy is called thus because only the faithful—those who have received baptism—may hear it. All others, unbelievers, catechumens—those who are preparing to receive the mystery of baptism—and penitents exit the temple. Therefore, right before the final portion of the Liturgy begins, the litany of the catechumens is exclaimed, during which the priest makes quiet intercession for them.

At the end of the litany [of the catechumens] the exclamation, "*Catechumens, depart...*" is pronounced from the ambo.[77] In ancient times, every catechumen exited the temple during this exclamation. Currently, this exclamation also has another meaning; it invites us to look within our own hearts—are they properly prepared to receive the coming Lord in the most sacred moment of the Liturgy?

---

[77] If a priest is serving without a deacon, the exclamation is made from the altar.

"*Catechumens, depart,*" now signifies for us the requirement to expel [from our hearts] every thought and everything earthly so as to meet the King of Glory.

Thoughts constantly master us. Some build in our souls a marketplace and there stir up noise and confusion, like at a bazaar; others engage in discussions and consultations and cause us to be scattered here, there, and everywhere. Another category of thoughts is those that burst in inadvertently and unnoticed. We must test ourselves: are we faithful to Christ, have we offended Him, or have we wandered away from Him?

Following this litany, those remaining prepare, with intensified prayer, for the approaching sacred moment of the Divine Service.

HOMILY 14

Let Us Stand Aright, Let Us Stand with Fear

That you may stand more easily and without distraction during the Divine Liturgy, do the following: while the hours are being chanted, remember the living and departed in your prayers. These commemorations will rise to heaven together with the commemorations being offered by the priest during the *proskomedia* and will bring great consolation to the souls of those remembered. Here it does not matter if the commemorations are made in the altar before the table of oblation, or at the doors of the altar, or in the midst of the church, for the Lord is everywhere and hears everything. When the opening exclamation of the Liturgy is made, "*Blessed is the Kingdom...*" pray that the Lord would grant unto you the Heavenly Kingdom. At the offering of the first litany of peace,[78] pray that the Lord would give you His peace during this day.

Nothing acts so favorably on the soul as a peaceful state, and so the enemy of salvation especially seeks to disturb

---

78 The Great Litany

it. He desires by every means—through quarrels, irritations, spite, frustrations, and grumbling—to lead a person out of a peaceful disposition and to destroy it. Therefore, when you pray for peace to be sent down into your soul, feel yourself as if but a small plank in the midst of raging waves, perceive your own feebleness and ask for help from the Lord. After this, the antiphons are sung. While they are sung, the priest offers prayers for the protection of the Church, and so you also should offer prayers to the Lord that He deliver this place in which you live from unbelief, heresy, and schism.

At the Little Entrance, the priest says the prayer, *"Grant that with our entrance there may be an entrance of Holy Angels ...."* During this time, the church is filled with a myriad of Holy Angels. And so, you should beseech your Guardian Angel that he stand beside you and pray with you, *"Holy Guardian Angel, have mercy on me and visit me."* While the apostolic Epistle and the Gospel are read, the angels, unseen by us, light countless candles. The priest prays, *"Illumine our hearts, O Master Who lovest mankind, with the pure light of Thy divine knowledge. Open the eyes of our minds to the understanding of Thy Gospel teachings ...."* At this moment, pray the Lord to send His Divine Light to you also, and that it would shine in your heart.

After this is the litany of fervent supplication—here the choir thrice repeats *"Lord have mercy"* after each supplication. This litany represents the entire earthly life of the Lord when great crowds followed after Him, crying out, "Lord have mercy on us!" Bring before your eyes this multitude—the Canaanite, the blind, and the lepers—and with all your soul fall down before the Lord; perceive yourself to be a leper, possessed, and blind. Mentally cling to the hem of the Lord's robe and entreat of Him mercy. Here it is good to bow yourself before an icon. The exclamation following the litany gives hope that the Lord will hear your cry, according to His great mercy: *"For Thou art a merciful God, Who lovest mankind, and to Thee we send up glory, to the Father, and to the Son, and to the Holy Spirit...."*

At the time of the litany of the catechumens, pray for all unbelievers. Maybe you have an acquaintance or family member who are unbelievers, pray that the Lord would have mercy and enlighten their souls with the light of faith. After this, give thanks to the Lord that by His providence you yourself are counted within the number of the faithful.

The Cherubic Hymn is the prayer of the Lord in Gethsemane. At this time, hold before your eyes the whole *podvig* of our Lord in Gethsemane—His prayer with sweat like great drops of blood and His suffering for people's sins. Remember that you came before the eyes of the Lord, with all your falls and sins. Feel deeply that on that night the Lord suffered for you. Especially acknowledge the fullness of your unworthiness—how could you repay the Lord for all He has done for you—and ask for His mercy. Remember how the Lord Himself was obedient to His Father's will, and so entrust yourself to the will of the Lord and resolve to patiently endure the crosses sent to you.

The time of the Great Entrance represents the Lord's crucifixion. Beseech Him to remember you in His Kingdom. At the exclamation, *"Peace be with you all,"* the Lord's descent into Hades, for the salvation of all the departed there before His coming, is depicted. Therefore, pray in this manner, *"Descend, O Lord, into the Hades of my soul and save me."* When you hear the exclamation, *"Let us love one another, that with one mind we may confess,"* pray that the Lord would plant in you holy love and give you to love everyone, most of all those that you do not love or have offended, and also those who do not love you and have offended you.

At the exclamation, *"Let us stand aright, let us stand with fear,"* pray that the Lord would plant in you His fear and that you would always remember the presence of the Lord. At the exclamation, *"Let us give thanks unto the Lord,"* offer up fervent thanksgiving. During this time, the priest reads a prayer in which all of the blessings of the Lord to mankind are remembered; so you also offer thanks for them and for the service of the Liturgy. At this point, everyone is obliged to give thanks for these things and in particular for the things given to him personally by the Lord, for all the mercies poured out on him. At the time of *"We praise Thee, we bless Thee..."* you should call to mind your sins, especially the serious ones and ask the Lord for forgiveness of them. In this manner, if you are diligently attentive to the Liturgy, then you will without fail receive great profit.

HOMILY 15

The Only True Foundation

On earth there is no greater treasure than the Divine Liturgy. Even if all the treasures of this world were gathered together, all the gold brought forth, every precious stone, every pearl taken from the oceans and the seas, and placed on one side of a scale, and on the other side is placed the Divine Liturgy—a Liturgy served by the simplest of village priests in the poorest of churches—the scale will tip toward the Divine Liturgy.

People do not understand or comprehend what treasure they possess. Until a happiness is removed, most people do not comprehend its value. Sadly, a person typically does not value that which he receives without labor—he does not value the sun or the air which he breathes. Only if the sun and air were somehow taken from him—if darkness were to descend and he had nothing to breathe—in that moment he would understand what he had and what he has lost.

And so it is with the Divine Liturgy. It is served daily and a person has the opportunity to be in church daily, and yet he does not go, or if he does go, he often is present but mentally distracted and carried about by the worries and cares of this life. Why is this? It comes from the fact that such a person does not contemplate upon the nature of the Divine Liturgy; he does not understand the whole depth and full significance of the service taking place before his eyes. Moreover, of all the miracles the greatest, most inscrutable, most wondrous of miracles is the Divine Liturgy, the Eucharist. For the sake of the Divine Liturgy the sun shines during the day, and the moon by night, and the heavenly stars shed forth their calm light, and the earth offers forth bread that it may become the Holy Lamb upon the altar. Only for the sake of the Divine Liturgy does the earth bring forth its fruit for bread, on which we feed—these are crumbs from the Lord's feast. [...][79] In the book of Revelation, St. John the Theologian outlines his vision, in which he beheld a woman clothed in the Sun of righteousness. And the dragon of the abyss strives to release his poison on her. The woman flees from him into the wilderness, but since the dragon pursues her even there, she hides in the rock[80] [...] According to the teaching of the Holy Fathers, the woman seen by St. John is the Church, clothed in the Sun of righteousness—Christ. In the last times, such a persecution will be raised against the Church that she will hide in the wilderness. The Divine Liturgy will be served underground. The Divine Liturgy will not be served on the land and the sun will not give its light and the earth will cease to give forth bread.[81]

The Divine Liturgy is the exact image of the earthly life of the Savior. It may be that you have a photograph of someone. When you look at it you can say, "How similar it is to the person—the eyes, the eyebrows, the nose—ev-

---

79 Indicates a break in original text
80 Cf. Revelation 12:13ff
81 Cf. Matthew 24:29

Homily 15: The Only True Foundation

erything is similar to the actual person." If a photograph is similar to your loved one then you endeavor to protect and keep it because it represents that person to you when you cannot see him. We can speak of the Divine Liturgy in a similar manner—it is an exact photograph and image of the whole earthly life of our Lord Jesus Christ. From Bethlehem, where the Pure Virgin came to be registered and give birth to the Lord, to the Jordan, and from the Jordan to Gethsemane, and from Gethsemane to Golgotha, and from Golgotha to Resurrection, and from Resurrection to the Mount of Olives—everything is visible in the Liturgy. And even if we are not among those blessed ones who lived during the time of our Lord's stay on earth, those who had the great joy of seeing Him face to face, yet we possess this priceless gift[82] that the Lord has left for us, and by which we are almost as fortunate as they were.

A mother sometimes leads her child by the hand, sometimes sits near him and observes him, and sometimes takes him up in her arms and caresses, cherishes, and nourishes him. In like manner, through every church service and home prayer, it is as though the Lord takes us by the hand and observes us from afar; in the Divine Liturgy, He takes us up in His arms, sits us together with Himself at the table, and feeds us at His Supper. In every service, except the Divine Liturgy, we speak with God as if over a telephone, but in the Divine Liturgy we speak with God face to face; we directly speak to the Lord about our needs and personally offer thanks and supplicate Him. Therefore, the prayers of the Divine Liturgy are more powerful than any other service. Thus, it is established that prayers for the departed be offered at the Divine Liturgy. By it, the souls of the departed are brought special consolation.

The Divine Liturgy is the window cut by the Lord Himself through which pure air comes into a sinful, unbe-

---

82 The Divine Liturgy

lieving, and adulterous world. If it were not for this window, believers would suffocate. The Divine Liturgy is the only true foundation according to which we must twine and weave the threads of our own lives. What else would you use to pattern your life? According to glory?[83] This is a foundation of clay. According to riches? This is a precarious foundation. Whatever else you may name, it does not matter, all of these things are precarious foundations of clay. The only true and mighty foundation is the Divine Liturgy.

Christians during the first centuries of Christianity attended the Divine Liturgy daily and communed of the Holy and Life-creating Mysteries of Christ. In those days, the lives of Christians were so holy and blameless, they lived so constantly present in God that their very lives were authentic preparation for the reception of the Holy Mysteries, and so no special preparation was demanded of them. If it happened that a Christian must be absent (from the Liturgy) or travel, then such a one—without exception, servant or lord, male or female—would take a small particle of the Holy Mysteries with himself and commune. Every Christian had the custom to bring three treasures with him (on a journey)—a cross, the Holy Gospel, and a vessel with a particle of the Holy Mysteries.

For the sake of the Divine Liturgy, Christians were ready to spill their blood and were persecuted by the pagans. They were tortured, crucified, burned, and often killed in the temple[84] itself—in the very catacombs during the service of the Eucharist. In ancient times, it was the custom to serve the Liturgy on the graves of martyred Christians; this was done as a sign of testimony to the great price at which the Divine Liturgy was purchased. Today,

---

83 Or fame

84 I.e., the Church building

Homily 15: The Only True Foundation

the memory of this is kept by sewing a portion of a relic from a saint into the *Antimins*.[85]

We will end our reflection on the meaning of the Divine Liturgy with this account of a vision that one ascetic-starets saw. He beheld a sea of fire with surging and boisterous waves; can you imagine such a terrible sight? On the other side upon the shore there stood a wonderful garden from which was heard the melodious song of birds and wafted the sweet scent of flowers. The ascetic heard a voice, "You must cross this sea." But it was impossible to cross. He stood long in thought about how he would cross it, and then he heard a voice, "Take up the two wings that are given in the Divine Eucharist: one wing is the Divine Body of Christ; the second wing is His Life-creating Blood. Without them it is impossible to reach the Kingdom of Heaven, no matter how great your *podvigs*." For this reason, Mary of Egypt, who offered *podvigs* for forty seven years, attaining even to being lifted into the air while at prayer, asked the holy elder Zosimus to add unto her this—the Holy and Life-creating Mysteries.

---

85 Or also spelled, *Antimension*. "The *Antimins* is a silk cloth consecrated by a bishop upon which Jesus Christ is depicted being placed in the tomb. Into the other side a fragment of the relics of a saint must be sewn, since in the first centuries of Christianity the Divine Liturgy was always celebrated upon the graves of the martyrs. One is not allowed to celebrate the Liturgy without *Antimins*. The word from the Greek means "instead of an altar table."" (Seraphim Slobodsky, *The Law of God*, (Jordanville: Holy Trinity Publications—Printshop of St. Job of Pochaev, 2013), 528.)

Homily 16— is the same as Homily 7.

HOMILY 17

The Fragrance of Christ

In today's Gospel reading,[86] we hear that after the entombment of Christ the Savior, the women who followed Christ—Mary Magdalene, Salome, and the others—prepared fragrant ointments because on the day after the Sabbath they desired to anoint the Most-Pure Body of the Lord. My friends, my beloved ones, my flock, these fragrant ointments have been safeguarded and kept even unto our day. We smell their blessed fragrance and also experience their comforting power; these ointments are nothing less than the Divine, mysterious, great, wondrous, beautiful, priceless, and healing Liturgy. Such is the fragrant ointment gifted to us by the first followers of the Lord! This is what we have received from them as an inheritance. This gift heals our wounds, cleanses the leprosy of our souls, and extinguishes the devouring flames of the passions. If we did not have this gift we would perish in this world full of impurity and every defilement, rotting alive and suffocating under its malevolence.

---

86 Most likely this refers to the reading from the Sunday of the Myrrh-bearing Women, Mark 15:43-16:8.

Homily 17: The Fragrance of Christ

I have already witnessed numerous times before you to this fact—if I, who am accursed and sinful, am still alive, if I still have breath, if I have not yet rotted away from the plague of sin, it is because I breathe in the miraculous fragrance of the Liturgy and my mouth is moistened with the Life-creating Blood of my Lord and Savior. The Divine Liturgy is the salt that safeguards me with its heavenly fragrance. It is my staff and it supports me and keeps me from falling; it is my anchor and it saves me from sinking; it is my sun and it illumines the gloomy abyss of my sins; it is my joy, delight, strength, and life. Here [on earth] I have only begun the Divine Liturgy but I will complete it there, in Heaven, with those children who have remained faithful with me, those who have attended the Divine Liturgy with me, loved it, and are nourished by this fragrant and life-creating fountain.

In the works of literary writers, the thoughts of the writer are not immediately revealed; sometimes a person must read the work for a while, until around the middle, to understand what it is that the author wants to say. The Holy Fathers acted in a similar manner when composing the Divine Liturgy. They take time to prepare the senses of the faithful to receive its most important parts. Calling the faithful to attention, the priest proclaims from the altar, "*The grace of our Lord Jesus Christ ....*" This pronounces the theme of the Divine Liturgy and here its whole meaning is summarized. What is the Liturgy? It is the grace, mercy, and gift of Christ Jesus. Consider, my dear ones, what joy it is to receive the grace of Christ the Savior, His gracious gift! We are graciously enveloped in the mercy of the Lord Jesus Christ. "*The love of God the Father*"—here again is what the Divine Liturgy is: love, the very sign of the Father's love.

"*God so loved the world that He gave His Only-Begotten Son, so that everyone who believes in Him should not perish but have eternal life.*"[87] The Liturgy bears witness to the Everlasting Love of God because it testifies above all else to this supreme sacrifice. How could you not cherish it? How could you not come to this supper of God's love?

"*The grace of our Lord Jesus Christ, the love of God the Father, and the communion of the Holy Spirit ....*"[88] Does not your soul tremble in awe upon hearing these words? You are communicants of God's Spirit, you are His kin, and you are partakers of His being. What joy, what a priceless gift we have in the Divine Liturgy! Through it we are made akin to the Comforter, God the Holy Spirit. Do not squander this gift from your God, take care of it! Diligently seek that the fragrance of this gift would envelop your soul and all of your life. If you neglect this fragrant flower of God, then you will rot in your own madness. Do you think that misfortune befalls us by chance? Is it a wonder that the worm devours our bread and winter corn?

No, it is not by mistake that this happens. Christians have forgotten about the fragrance of Christ, they have forgotten about the Divine Liturgy. On a feast day, instead of going to church, they go to the market, to the field, to chop wood, and to take up the scythe. I would not be surprised if nothing will be left in our fields because we have angered the Lord by neglecting His gift.

As long as we remain in the fragrance of the Divine Liturgy, as long as we are Christ's, we ourselves are blessed; we partake of the good and then are able to give good to others. We bear on ourselves a seal, the seal of the love of God; we are akin to the Comforter, the Holy Spirit, and then are able to give comfort to others. If we turn away from Christ and do not attend the Divine Liturgy, then we will lose this gift of God; then we will receive an-

---

87 John 3:16. Similar wording is also used in the second anaphora prayer.

88 The priestly exclamation before the anaphora prayers

Homily 17: The Fragrance of Christ

other gift—not from Christ but from the antichrist, from Satan—because wherever Christ is absent, there is not simply emptiness, no, there the gift of Satan is made. He is not the giver of good but a giver of evil, and he plants malice and enmity into the hearts of his followers. Instead of the shining grace and love of God the Father, there reigns in them dark demonic hatred, and rather than being made communicants of God they become the communicants of Satan. Woe to the person who permits him even near himself.

For this reason, I am constantly calling you to the Divine Liturgy. It pours out goodness on the world; it is eternal love and the presence of the Holy Spirit. Yet, some people are not thankful for this priceless gift of God; they consider missing the service of God, for no good reason, to be of trivial importance. Do they not understand that after the first and second absence, they begin to grow accustomed to being absent? Then little by little in place of the gracious and kindred Holy Spirit, they become cruel and akin to the spirit of darkness. This is why the ancient Church excommunicated those who missed three consecutive Sunday Liturgies.

"O Lord, give Thy grace and love to those children of mine who love Thy Liturgy, and grant that they may be with me there [in Heaven] where I will complete it!"

HOMILY 18

Let Us Lift Up Our Hearts

My friends, my dear ones, there was a fearfully deep and horrible abyss. It was pitch black and not one single ray of sun broke its gloom; it was suffocating and not one little gust of fresh air ever stirred in it; it was full of creeping things, snakes, and stench. In this abyss prisoners languished, they languished in misery and sorrow. Suddenly a magnificent and mighty eagle flew into this abyss. He stretched out his two great wings and cried out, "All of you miserable and suffocating prisoners who are languishing in this abyss, take hold of my wings, hold on tightly to them, and I will carry you up into the heights, even to the sun!" The prisoners believed the eagle and took hold of his mighty wings, holding tightly, and the mighty eagle carried them out of the abyss. Higher and higher he carried those who clung to his wings. Already the expanse of the earth could be seen, and he climbed higher still! They asked the eagle, "Thank you, we now see the whole dear world. Where else are you taking us?" "Only hold on tightly and I will carry you higher still, to the very sun!" And he began ascending higher and higher. Up past heaven, past

Homily 18: Let Us Lift Up Our Hearts

the shining and radiant luminaries; he flew to the second heaven, then to the third, and to the heaven of heavens but he did not stop even there; he ascended to the very throne of the Eternal Sun and here before the face of the Almighty he set down everyone he was carrying.

My friends, this eagle is Christ our Savior. The abyss from which He delivered us is Hades, where all those under the Old Testament were imprisoned, languishing under the bonds and chains of Satan—the prophets and righteous ones and all the departed. To these sorrowful ones, the eagle descended because the texts of the Holy Scriptures call Him an eagle.[89]

Our Risen Lord descended even to these sufferers, during which time no one on earth yet knew of His Resurrection, for the dawn was just breaking on the Day of Resurrection. I have already said that the exclamations, *"Through the compassions of Thine Only-begotten Son ...,"* *"Peace be unto all,"* and *"Let us love one another..."* signify the first proclamation of the Resurrection in Hades.[90] The singing of the Symbol of Faith represents the delight of those in Hades who were the first to receive this proclamation (of the Resurrection). The exclamation *"Let us lift up our hearts"* is the appearing of the Deliverer Himself in Hades. He appeared and shattered the gloomy abyss of Hades; He appeared and its gates crumbled for all eternity! All of those resurrected stood on its gates, trampling them and their bonds underfoot, as it is depicted in the fresco at the Church in Chora.[91]

First, the Lord called to fallen Adam and he took hold of His mighty wing—the hand of the Savior—and clung to it with the delight of thanksgiving, and on the other

---

89 Cf. Psalm 90/91:1-4; Exodus 19:4

90 The reality of the Resurrection was manifested to those in Hades before it was revealed to those on earth.

91 A famous fresco depicting the Resurrection

hand clung Eve. She fell prostrate before the Deliverer, daring not even to look on Him. Then came the prophets and the other righteous ones of the Old Testament *"in joyful step, praising the eternal Pascha."*[92]

And so, this leading of the departed out of Hades is commemorated in the exclamation, *"Let us lift up our hearts."* But now there is also another Hades—fearful, gloomy, terrible, and unbearably heavy—the Hades of the soul. This is when the soul is engulfed in the grief of loneliness, for it seems that you are forgotten by everyone and abandoned; it is also when the soul is weighed down in the abyss of the passions, those creeping serpents of our life. Into this abyss of despair and sin flies the Eagle—the Savior—and lifts up our souls on His mighty wings and carries us to the Never-setting Sun. These wings are the Most-Pure Body of Christ and His Life-creating Blood. Who has not known this Hades of the soul? Who has not lived through times of complete despair, and feelings of total abandonment? And yet, after communing of the Life-creating Mysteries of Christ, who has not received grace-filled help and healing? These all-healing Holy Mysteries we receive at the Divine Liturgy. How thankful we must be to the Lord for this priceless gem that has been given to us. St. John Chrysostom says that even if we were never able to taste of the Holy Mysteries, and were only able to gaze upon them as they were carried before our eyes, even then we must give thanks to the Lord. But we have been granted to taste of them!

My lips just received the Holy Body and my tongue was just moistened with the Life-creating Mysteries! I call to you my poor and sorrowful friend—sinful, weak, wallowing in the passions, and exhausted in the battle with temptation—come here to the Holy Chalice and be strengthened because here is strength; come here and be

---

92 Ode 5 of the Paschal Canon, St John of Damascus

Homily 18: Let Us Lift Up Our Hearts

reborn because here is life; come here and be enlightened because here is light; come here and leave behind your falls into Hades, even if you have fallen into the very claws of Satan. Only come here because here is salvation. Only do not tarry, only do not neglect the greatest gifts of God, only cry with contrition, "Have mercy on me!" Have faith that you will be heard. Only rise up from worldly cares and vanities that are so full of lust and impurity. Lift up your heart on high, take hold of the Savior's two wings, and come to the pure spring of the Divine Liturgy.

The Holy Fathers knew the great power of the Divine Liturgy and proclaimed their awe before it. When the venerable Father Seraphim[93] was infirm and someone said that it must be hard for him to attend the Liturgy, he answered, "Yes, but even if I had no strength to walk at all, I would crawl there on my hands and knees."

"*Let us lift up our hearts*"—lift up unto the heights, lift up your heart above everything earthly. This exclamation calls us to carry our hearts high above everything lowly and earthly and to lift our thoughts to the heights as we stand before the most important moment of the Liturgy. At this moment, at least forget about the daily vanities and cares of this life. Be like an angel, full of thoughts only about God and service to Him. Behold here and now He is present and blesses you.

The venerable Father Seraphim beheld the Lord Jesus Christ, surrounded by the hosts of heavenly powers, come from the western door and walk to the eastern door. With His outstretched arms He blessed all those gathered in prayer, covering them with His hands as with wings. Many other saints have beheld Him too. The ancient Christians beheld Him and felt His presence. Only we with our earthbound hearts, which we never lift up to the heavens, only we do not behold Him. But it is worth our while to at least

---

[93] Of Sarov

raise ourselves up a little bit above our earthly cares—then we will feel His closeness. This is why at the call to "lift up," the ancient Christians, all together, however many were gathered in the temple, exclaimed, "*We lift them up to the Lord*"—we lift up our hearts to the Lord! Today only the choir responds.

The call to "lift up our hearts" prepares us for the most majestic portion of the Divine Liturgy, which begins with the exclamation "*Let us give thanks to the Lord*" and is completed with the exclamation, "*And grant that with one mouth and one heart.*" This section is called the Eucharist canon or the Eucharistic portion. "Eucharist" is from a Greek word that means, "thanksgiving." "Canon" means "rule" or "standard." In that sense, this part is called the standard of thanksgiving. This is because, specifically, at this point of the Divine Liturgy thanksgiving is offered up to the Lord for the greatest of His gifts. It is called the Eucharistic portion because it is distinguished by very extended chanting during which time the priest quietly recites long and tender prayers. The Eucharistic canon is the most important, the most moving, and the most fearful part of the Divine, mystical, wondrous, great, and Most-holy Liturgy. It is the heart of the Liturgy. And remarkably, this portion has been preserved for us as the Lord Jesus Christ Himself instituted it at the Mystical Supper, as it was composed by the Apostles: James, who first wrote the hymns for the Divine Liturgy; Paul, who wrote prayers for it, which he heard from the angels themselves; and the seer of mysteries, John the Theologian.

The other parts of the Liturgy—the *proskomedia*, the Liturgy of the Catechumens, and the Liturgy of the Faithful—all of them have undergone a number of alterations and reductions. Only the Eucharistic canon has remained unchanged. The hands of later writers in the Holy Church did not touch its divinely inspired prayers. In all the Chris-

Homily 18: Let Us Lift Up Our Hearts

tian world <...>[94] this canon has preserved the ancient structure.

The Eucharistic canon is composed of six parts: 1) the glorification of God, 2) the hymn of the Seraphim (the Triumphant Hymn), 3) the elevation of the Gifts, 4) the blessing of the Gifts, 5) the commemoration of the saints, 6) the completion of the canon, the conclusion.

The first part of the Eucharistic canon is the glorification, during which we glorify and give thanks to the Lord for His mercy towards us. *"Let us give thanks unto the Lord,"* exclaims the priest from the altar and from the ambo the hierarch covers in blessing the gathered worshippers with the *dikirion* and *trikirion* candles. The believers respond and sing, *"It is meet and right...."* <...> As you see, here the properties of God are indicated—God, Who is ineffable. Of especial significance is the name of God - "I AM." In the Old Testament, the Lord called Himself by this mysterious and great name when Moses asked the burning bush, "When they ask me what is His name? What shall I say?" God answered, "Tell them, I AM, for I am your Lord" (cf. Exodus 3:13-15). In Hebrew, I AM is "Yehovah."[95] This name has great meaning; it means that only God truly Is—always and for eternity. If we live, move, and have being, it is only because He has deigned it to be so for us. Without Him we are nothing; if God were not, then neither would we exist, nor would our earth and the whole world around us.

"Ever existing and eternally the same,"[96] this expression sounds like an oath. It demonstrates that we confess this property of God to be an immutable truth. This very God Who Is has granted the priest to offer thanks, "Thou and

---

94   Indicates a break in the original text
95   Jehovah or Yahweh
96   Words from the first Anaphora prayer

Thine Only-begotten Son and Thy Holy Spirit." <...> For this we offer thanks to the Lord and finally we give thanks that He accepts our human service before the Chalice, even though there stand before Him thousands upon thousands of heavenly powers. Yet, the Son of God did not redeem them with His Blood, He did not come to purchase them; rather, He came for us, the sinful and weak ones.

This giving of thanks is even better expressed by St. Basil the Great, whose Liturgy is longer than that of St. John Chrysostom. Due to human weakness and so to give everyone the opportunity to be present at the Liturgy, it was shortened over time. The Liturgy of St. Basil the Great is now served only ten times in a year. <...> This is how the Lord is glorified in the first part of the Eucharistic canon. It shows to us how we must raise our hearts up in prayer. *"Let us lift up our hearts"*—to offer thanksgiving and to glorify the Lord.

I, the weak one, the worst of sinners, again and again call to you with my mouth that is moistened with the Divine Blood—come to the Liturgy! Understand this—whatever is done during the time when the Liturgy is offered, whatever is done not due to need or obligation but simply because you did not feel like coming to the service, will not work for your good because it is completely rotten from the start and devoid of God's grace.

HOMILY 19

Holy, Holy, Holy, Lord of Sabaoth

Last time I explained the first part of the Eucharistic canon, which is called the glorification. The second part is called the hymn of the Seraphim. My friends, we are willing to devote a lot of time to the thorough study of the writings of famous authors. If we are willing to give so much attention to the works of the human mind, which is rotting, always imperfect, and nothing, then how much more diligently, thoroughly, and attentively should we study the works and creations of a mind established by the Holy Spirit.

What grateful delight, what holy trembling should seize our souls when we pronounce the name "Hymn of the Seraphim." It is the song of the Seraphim who are the closest to the Throne of the Almighty, and who are aflame with the fire of God's love, as it is written in one holy text. The Seraphim's love is a fiery flame. These fiery servants of the Lord unceasingly glorify Him and never grow tired of singing, "*Holy, Holy, Holy, Lord of Sabaoth, heaven and earth are full of Thy glory.*"[97]

---

97 Cf. Rev. 4:8

Who heard this miraculous song, what composer gave us this heavenly music? Five people, my beloved ones, have heard this heavenly song; five composers reproduced the words of the fiery Seraphim—three are from the Old Testament, and two are from the New. The divine Isaiah heard the song of the Seraphim as he rapturously proclaimed the Divine Liturgy of the Old Testament. In the sixth chapter of his book, he tells us the Seraphim cover their faces in awe, not daring to gaze upon the face of God. How much more awe should we have when He grants us not only to see but also partake of Him with our very own mouths in the Mystery of Holy Communion. Contemplate on what a great mercy of God is revealed to us at this time!

The devout Ezekiel was the second one to hear the hymn of the Seraphim and see them. He beheld the Throne of the Lord supported by the four living-creatures, which are now depicted around the four Evangelists.[98] In remembrance of these living-creatures, these words are proclaimed during the Divine Liturgy, "*Singing the triumphant hymn, shouting, proclaiming, and saying.*" Singing relates to the eagle, shouting to the bull, proclaiming—or in the Greek "roaring" - to the lion, and saying to the man. At the proclamation of these words the deacon taps the *diskos* four times with the star in remembrance of the voices of the living-creatures, who support the Throne of the Lord of Hosts.

The third one to behold the glory of God was the man of desire, the prophet Daniel. The Ancient of Days was seated on a Throne and thousands of thousands, innumerable myriads, attended to Him. A river of fire flowed before Him.[99]

---

98 Cf. Ezekiel. 1:4ff

99 Cf. Daniel 7:9-10

In the New Testament the divine apostle Paul beheld the Lord, for he was lifted up to the third heaven and heard ineffable words that are impossible for anyone to utter.[100]

And finally, John the Theologian, the seer of mysteries and apostle, while on an island[101] saw the Lord in the image of the majestic Son of Man and recorded this vision in his Revelation. It is he who told the apostle James and the other authors of the Divine Liturgy of the Seraphic hymn. You, my friends, just meditate on whose hymn we are singing—that of the Seraphim and of the angels. This one name has already sanctified our mouths—do not imagine that it means nothing when we pronounce the name of angels, the saints, the Most-Sweet name of the Lord Jesus Christ, and the Most-Pure Theotokos. No, in saying their names we are not simply pronouncing words because if they are pronounced with due attention and reverence, they sanctify us and call upon us the grace-filled mercy and help of the One Whose name we pronounce, *"Lord Jesus Christ, have mercy on me a sinner," "Most-Holy Theotokos save us."* Pronouncing them first with our mouths, they then pass over to the heart. But we do not pronounce them as we should and this is why we do not sense the grace-filled action of these words on us. Maybe if we would at least call on them as fervently as we call for our cattle that have yet to return home, even then we would feel the power of these holy names. But we don't even do that. Our cold mouths do not raise our words of prayer up to the saints, nor do they unite us to them.

"Holy, Holy, Holy," sing the Seraphim day and night; with two of their wings they cover their faces, so reverent are they before the Almighty that they dare not count themselves worthy to gaze on the holy countenance of the

---

100 Cf. 2 Cor. 12:1-4

101 Patmos

Lord. With two wings they cover their feet and with two wings they fly. As the faithful in the temple are repeating the Seraphic glorification, the priest quietly prays, *"With these blessed powers ...."* This prayer explains why we must give thanks to the Lord and why the Seraphim unceasingly sing to Him, *"Holy art Thou and All-Holy."* The Father so loved the world to give His Only-begotten Son that whosoever believes in Him should not perish[102]—this is the reason for such exultation in heaven and such trembling reverence.

The Lord is the Creator of the world and the luminous spirits[103]; the Lord Almighty and Fearsome, upon Whom the celestial ones dare not gaze. He it is Who so loved the world—sinful and impure, full of sin, evil, and lusts, full of filth—this world He so loved that He gave His Only-begotten Son for its salvation. Think on this, my friends, He gave His Son! And this Son came preaching peace and love but those to whom He came hung Him on the Cross, they condemned Him to unbearable torment, and betrayed Him to death. The heavens shuttered and the Cherubim were astounded with perplexity. The Thrones, Dominions, Powers, Principalities, Archangels, and Angels stood in fear and bewilderment. The Only- begotten Son, before Whom they stand with reverence—He is humiliated and crushed and dies on the Cross. The famous artist Vasnetsov[104] amazingly depicts this in a painting that carries the name "So loved the world." The sky is covered in dark clouds, from which it seems peals of thunder sound; zigzags of fiery lightning pierce the darkness that shrouds the earth and illuminates the Cross, and on a Throne above the clouds the Ancient of Days looks upon the earth. Be-

---

102 Cf. John 3:16

103 I.e., the Angels

104 Viktor Vasnetsov, 1848-1926

fore Him throng the Seraphim in reverent fear, struck with amazement, one of whom extends to Him his hands in complete wonder at the mystery, which is inscrutable even for his shining intellect. The other one clings to the arm of the Lord of Hosts, full of awe he has even ceased singing and the festal hymn has fallen silent for a time. The other two Seraphim prostrate themselves before the Throne and are enveloped in the clouds like a soaring eagle is enveloped in the blue sky. *"God so loved the world that He gave His Only-begotten Son, so that everyone who believes in Him should not perish."*[105]

My friends, my dearly loved ones, do you understand these words "God so loved the world"? And His Son full of the same love descended to the earth, took the form of a servant, received every humiliation, and finally died a shameful death.[106] And not only that; He, the Only-begotten Son of God, Consubstantial with the Father, on that night took bread, broke and gave it, saying, *"Take, eat;"* He gave the cup saying, *"Drink of it, all of you."* In this way He communed His disciples and has also given these priceless gifts to us who believe in Him. We eat His Body and drink His Blood.[107]

Our impure and wicked mouths are moistened with His Blood. This Divine gift permeates our very being and passes into every one of our members. He has given us the Divine Liturgy at which the mystery of the Dread Sacrifice is always offered. So great is God's love toward us, so infinite, that it encompasses the whole world, every creature, and all of creation. It is only because this Sacrifice is offered up that the earth gives forth fruit. The earth was subjected to a curse, under which it brings forth weeds. If

---

105 John 3:16

106 Philippians 2:5ff

107 Cf. John 6:53-57

we eat bread, it is only because it is needed for the Divine Liturgy, only because every day it is set forth on the table of oblation and the altar in remembrance of the slain Lamb, and every day the Mystery of the Dread Sacrifice is served. As long as the Divine Liturgy is served, I will fear nothing—neither hunger, nor pestilent insects, nor drought, nor hailstorms. I know that bread is needed for the Liturgy and the earth will bring it forth. Even if the sky turns to brass and the earth becomes dry and hardened, still I would not fear that we will perish. No! The Sacrifice is offered and the priest exclaims, *"Thine own of Thine own!"* The earth will give what is needed at the lifting up and offering of these words. Fear nothing! Hope in God, Who so loved the world.

But woe if the Divine Liturgy ceases to be served; woe if the Bloodless Sacrifice is not offered. Then the world will perish. The earth will not give fruit because it is subject to a curse and is living only thanks to His unspeakable love, and it serves Him with bread. [If the Divine Liturgy ceases] the sun will no longer give its light because it is needed for the bringing forth of bread in the service of the Divine Liturgy; we will, all of us, die because we live only through Christ our Lord. But I believe the Liturgy will not cease to be served and the Seraphim will join with people and eternally sing, *"Holy, Holy, Holy, Lord of Sabaoth."*

HOMILY 20

Take, Eat

Today I desire to spend more time examining the second part of the Eucharistic canon, the Seraphic Hymn. What do the words of this short hymn mean, that which the Holy Prophet Isaiah heard in his wondrous vision, "*Holy, Holy, Holy*"? I think everyone understands these words and it is clear why they are repeated three times. In the Old Testament, we frequently encounter indications of the Three Persons of the Holy Trinity. The Seraphic Hymn confesses this, the greatest of our dogmas. The word "Sabaoth" requires some explanation. The translation of the Hebrew word "Sabaoth" means "*Lord of the armies.*"[108] Great is this title. You should ponder it. God is called the "Lord of the armies." This is, first of all, because He is the creator of the heavenly armies.

But such a name also means that the Lord especially blesses, especially protects, all those who wage war in His Name, and those who battle with their passions, the devil,

---

[108] Or may also be translated as "Lord of Hosts." Both of these possible translations will be used throughout this homily.

and this adulterous and evil world; those who stand up and defend the Name of the Lord against His enemies.

The Lord does not love a weak, timid, and sluggish spirit. He requires us to courageously and steadfastly confess Him. God's Church glorifies enlighteners, righteous and venerable ones, and yet the Lord promises a particularly high reward to the martyrs who endured physical and bodily torments for Him, together with those who endure spiritual torments—ridicule, persecution, harassment, and slander—because they glorify His name. And so, they teach us that we should stand fearlessly and firmly in defense of His Church, that we should not fear sufferings and persecutions in the defense of her statutes, foundations, and dogmas. They courageously endured every temptation and attack from the enemy, especially from the servants of the prince of darkness; they steadfastly and persistently fought against sin and their own passions. Such strong warriors the Lord especially covers with His Grace; with exceptional attention He expressly seeks for such persons, and they receive His tender mercy. As an earthly commander cares for his soldiers and knows each one by face and their needs, so does the Lord of the armies; the Lord is the Heavenly Commander and He cares for and knows by face each of His warriors. All of His prophets, all of His apostles, are at the same time His warriors. Each of them carried out intense warfare and suffered martyrdom for the confession of His Name. With what love, attention, and protection the Lord embraces His servants, those who are of His army.

Thus, my dear ones, when you sing these words "Holy, Holy, Holy," pray that the Lord would give you fortitude in the battle with sin and that He would strengthen you to joyfully stand in His fearful Name. When you sing the words, "Holy, Holy, Holy," look inside yourself and discern who are you: a servant and warrior of the Heavenly King, one courageously and valiantly advancing on the enemy, the devil, or are you a defector who has fled the battlefield and shamefully run away from the battle standard of your Commander?

Never forget to correctly and firmly hold the sword of the Lord—His Cross. The sign of His Cross confounds enemies both visible and invisible. Clothe yourself, as the apostle says, in the full armor of Salvation.[109] Stand bravely and defend God's Church and the Lord's Holy Name. The Lord of Hosts, Who dwells in the host of His martyrs, ascetics, and those battling the passions, will send you special grace. The next words, *"Heaven and earth are full of Thy glory,"* are quite understandable. They mean exactly heaven and earth are full of Thy glory, the whole world shows forth the glory of God.

The next word is "Hosanna." I want you to understand this word. "Hosanna"—in Hebrew it is *hosha'na* and in Greek, *ossana*, which is a greeting: "Greetings to you!" "May good come upon you!" In such a manner, this word may be translated. Every nation gives expression to their joy and special exclamations when greeting prominent figures, such as leaders. The Hebrews expressed their feelings in this word—hosha'na. In the Old Testament Church, there was celebrated the feast of Tabernacle; during this feast the Jews would go into the fields and build booths from green boughs and live in them throughout the celebration.[110] The Hebrew children, taking branches in their hands, would greet each other in the fields with the waving of these branches and the cry *hosha'na*—hosanna—that is, "we greet you," "greetings of good," and "may you have joy!" With these exclamations, the children (particularly)

---

109 Cf. Ephesians 6:10ff

110 Cf. Leviticus 23:33ff

went out to meet Christ the Savior as He entered Jerusalem.

Our singing of *"Hosanna in the highest, blessed is He who comes..."* expresses our greeting of the coming Christ. The Seraphim, beholding his unending love for people and beholding Him coming to sacrifice, greet Him with trembling awe; the whole world echoes their greeting, all of nature, everything glorifies Him. Why does the whole world bring praise to the Lord? The quiet priestly prayer clarifies this. As those gathered in the temple sing, "Holy, Holy, Holy"—the Seraphic hymn—the priest prays, *"With these blessed powers..."* which ends with, *"Take, eat."* Here is the greatest good that the Lord has given us—the Divine Liturgy. This is why the trembling cloud of Seraphim flock to the temple. These powers always stand with trembling reverence before the Lord's Throne; they are always in a state of awe and delight of love. But what of us, the people, to whom this good is given? We depart from it and rarely attend the Liturgy; rather we exchange it for the market and earthly cares. My friends, fear this! Fear to lose the blessing that is given. If we lose it, we lose everything because it is the fountain of our life. It is the axis upon which turns the wheel of our life.

This is what I wanted to tell you in today's discourse. Now, I also desire to touch upon the Gospel that we heard today and which I find so touching. The Gospel tells of Christ's appearance to two apostles on the road to Emmaus.[111] At first they did not know Jesus; it was only when He took bread and broke and gave it to them that their eyes were opened and they knew the Lord. This appearance of the Lord speaks to us of the Divine Liturgy. For here, the Lord also appears openly under the forms of bread and wine, and only in the mystery of Holy Communion does He disclose Himself to us. The very actions that

---

111 Cf. Luke 24:13ff

Homily 20: Take, Eat

the Lord performed are repeated in the Liturgy, wherein bread and wine are also blessed, broken, and given to the communicants. Only in the breaking of the bread did the disciples recognize the Lord and precisely in the Divine Liturgy may we know Him. The apostles asked when the Lord left them, *"Were not our hearts burning within us while He spoke to us?"*[112] And our hearts are set aflame by the fire of Holy Communion.

Therefore, love the Holy Liturgy because the Peaceful Light of Christ is reflected in it; love it because in the Liturgy you may uniquely behold and experience Christ.

---

112 Luke 24:32

HOMILY 21

The Elevation of the Holy Gifts

My dear ones, once there were two families who lived in an immensely large home. Yet, between the two there was a huge difference in the manner of their lives: one family dwelt in the bright and sunny side of the house while the other family dwelt in its dark side. On the side where the first family lived, there was a large bright window through which radiant rays of light shone; it was clean, had fresh air, and treated the eyes to an exquisite view. The space itself, thanks to the light and air, was completely suitable for healthy living—it was dry, warm, and clean. The people living there were always in good health and cheerful. But on the other side of the house there was no window and it was gloomy, dark, and cold. Most importantly, there constantly arose harmful vapors and stenches because this side was next to a low swampy place. The people who dwelt on this side of the house were frequently sick; they were pale, sluggish, and cheerless.

My friends, this home represents our world. The bright window on the first side of the house is the Divine Liturgy. I, a sinner, dare to say that in this bright service—

Homily 21: The Elevation of the Holy Gifts

in this window—is open to me such a miraculous, such a wondrous view of eternal blessedness that it seems my heart cannot contain its feelings of supreme thankfulness to God, Who has sent us such a gift!

Those who dwell in the bright side are those who have faith in Christ, come to the Divine Liturgy, breathe of the fragrance of God's grace—poured out through this service—and enjoy the warmth of love and light from the Sun of Righteousness. Such people are healthy of spirit, bright, and peaceful because they are covered with the healing power of the Holy Spirit. Those who dwell in the dark part are those who do not desire to be with Christ and do not treasure the Holy Liturgy. These pitiful people do not experience the warmth and grace of Christ the Savior. Their life is full of stench and rot because the vaporous and foul passions blind their souls. They have no window or ventilation by which to purify this rottenness from their souls; that is why, sometimes, the life of such people is so dark and gloomy. For this reason, my dear ones, I call you to come to the Divine Liturgy; for this reason I so desire that you would comprehend and love it—the light that illumines even the darkest abyss of sin. It is warmth that thaws even the most icy-cold soul; it is love, joy, and life.

Today I desire to explain to you the third portion of the Eucharistic canon—the elevation of the Holy Gifts. Yet, at the moment, I want to once again focus your attention on the Seraphic Hymn, namely on the quiet priestly prayer offered during the hymn, and specifically as it is said in the Liturgy of St. Basil the Great. This prayer is a comprehensive and fiery hymn to the Lord, Creator, and Fashioner, Who has poured out on people His measureless mercy. Here every word is a work of the deepest wisdom and grace.

It is no wonder that St. Basil the Great prepared for the composition of the Divine Liturgy with long prayer and fasting, and only then in the ecstasy of fiery prayer while prostrate before the altar did he compose these incredible prayers and write them down. These prayers are in the second part of the Eucharistic canon. Doubtlessly, St. Basil derived these prayers from the fiery Seraphim themselves, for they concelebrated together with this wondrous man. *"With these blessed powers... Holy art Thou—truly Most Holy...."*[113] Once again, pay attention to the word "truly;" once again a sworn assurance is given here to the truth of what is being confessed. *"Most Holy, and there are no bounds to the magnificence of Thy holiness."*[114]

Further, this magnificence is explained, for it is the great beauty of God, *"With righteousness ... Thou hast created man;"*[115] thus the creation of mankind is outlined—his blessedness and his fall into sin and the promised salvation, *"Providing for him the salvation of regeneration in Thy Christ Himself."*[116] Pay attention—*"salvation... in Thy Christ Himself."* This is the foundation stone of our faith. And then, at length, the many mercies of God to the sinful human race are enumerated. *"Thou didst send prophets,"* and further on these words, *"When the fullness of time had come,"* and this is speaking, as you see, about Christ, Who *"emptied Himself, taking the form of a servant,"*[117] and behold what a detailed confession of the God-Man's deep humility and condescension follows together with the purpose of His coming into the world! *"He appeared on earth... He obtained us for His chosen people, a royal priesthood, a holy nation."*[118] Do you hear who we are, thanks to the sacrifice of Christ? A

---

113 From the second Anaphora prayer of St. Basil the Great
114 Ibid.
115 Ibid.
116 Ibid.
117 Ibid. Also, cf. Phil. 2:6-7
118 Ibid. Also, cf. 1 Peter 2:9

royal priesthood, a holy nation! "Having cleansed us" who were "sold under sin" (the devil completed a purchase, he purchased us through sin)[119] and behold, Christ descended *"through the Cross into Hades" and "made for all flesh a path."* As I have said before,[120] Christ flew down into Hades on behalf of every one of us, and *"made a path for all flesh, a path to the resurrection from the dead."*[121]

And further the Resurrection and the coming Judgment are spoken of. The whole history of mankind, from creation until the last Judgment, is deeply outlined in such a concise, clear, and exact manner. At the end of the prayer, the closing words *"He has left us these things"* indicate the transition to the third part of the Eucharistic canon and the elevation of the Holy Gifts. During the Liturgy of St. John Chrysostom, this transition takes place at the words, *"When He had come and fulfilled..."*[122] and then the words, *"Take, eat."* The priest loudly proclaims these words and they must be received as the very words of the Lord Jesus Christ Himself. He Himself calls to us with the very most-holy and most-precious words that He pronounced on the night of His sufferings. Surely we will not remain deaf to this Divine call; at that time, those gathered in church answer this call from Christ the Savior with a twofold amen, which is to say, "true and faithful." The priest quietly reads [the prayer] *"Remembering this saving commandment..."*[123] and finishes this short prayer with the exclamation, *"Thine own of Thine own."* The Liturgy of St. Basil includes the words, *"This do in remembrance of Me."*

---

119 Cf. Roman 7:14, 23-24

120 Cf. Homily 18

121 From the second Anaphora prayer of St. Basil the Great

122 From the second Anaphora prayer of St. John Chrysostom

123 The priestly prayer before the elevation of the Holy Gifts

That the words *"Take, eat"* are pronounced by the Lord Jesus Christ Himself is made even clearer in the service of the hierarchical Liturgy. Have you ever noticed that at the reading of the Gospel the bishop removes the *omophorion*?[124] I will tell you what the *omophorion* is—the most loved garment of the Savior. It represents the lost sheep that the Good Shepherd takes on His shoulders. In removing the *omophorion* from the bishop, he stands as a simple servant of the altar because it means in that moment the Lord is not speaking through him to the people, but rather the Lord is directly speaking to the people through the Gospel. Yet, before the elevation of the Holy Gifts, the small omophorion is once again placed on the bishop's shoulders. He is now not a mortal, sinful, and weak servant of the altar. No, before the altar stands the Lord Himself. The bishop represents His most-holy image and His voice calls to us, *"Take!"* Be attentive to the words of your Savior, hearken to them with fearful reverence; at least for this short moment forget about all worldly squabbles, every strife, and daily care.

The words *"Take, eat..."* indicate the third portion of the Eucharistic canon—the elevation of the Holy Gifts. Having remembered the Divine words spoken by the Divine Teacher at the Mystical Supper, the priest then takes in his hands the Holy Chalice and *Diskos* and lifting them up on high, he proclaims, *"Thine own of Thine own, we offer unto Thee, on behalf of all and for all."* The choir sings, *"We praise Thee, We bless Thee...."* "Thine," the priest pronounces, showing the bread and wine to the Lord, as if to say, "Thine—Thy gifts, the fruits of the earth, which are given to us, we bring to Thee." I will repeat it again, however many times I must tell you, for this reason alone does the earth bring forth fruit—wheat and grapes; for this alone she rewards us for our labors, so that everyday bread

---

124 The distinctive vestment of Bishops in the Orthodox Church

and wine are offered on the Holy Altar during the Divine Liturgy. No, not for us sinners who are covered with the wounds of sin, not for us does the earth give forth her fruit because we are unworthy of them, she gives them for the Bloodless Sacrifice and will continue to give them as long as the dread and Holy Liturgy is served on earth.

"Thine own of Thine own," that is, from Thy slaves, from Thy people, *"we offer unto Thee,"* and we offer, *"on behalf of all and for all." "On behalf of all,"* may be explained thus, on behalf of every sin and for every iniquity. What a great, what a blessed phrase is *"on behalf of all!"* On behalf of everyone, for every sin this Sacrifice is offered; every iniquity is washed in the Blood that is poured out for us. O, impoverished sinner, covered in sins like leprosy, who has fallen into the abyss of the passions, O sinner, lift up your head, strengthen yourself with hope because through God's endless love for mankind the Mystical Sacrifice is also lifted up on behalf of your sins and unrighteousness. O, what a joyful promise! Such a gift we have in the Divine Liturgy! *"And for all"*—these words express thanksgiving to the Lord for all His mercies to us.

We are offering to Thee Thine own gifts, for the earth is Thine, on behalf of Thy servants and for redemption from all their sins, and in thanksgiving for all the great mercies and blessings toward us. Such is the meaning of this exclamation.

Now, let us look at how the priest holds the Holy Chalice and *Diskos*—he crosses his right hand over his left and raises the Holy Gifts on high. He, as it were, covers himself with the sign of the cross. What a deep meaning is found here! The priest is a man—he is a sinner like everyone else and maybe worse than everyone else—and he dares to offer the dread Sacrifice before which the very Seraphim tremble, and they are the very first of the angelic ranks who stand before the very Throne of God! The priest dares draw near to the Holy Altar, upon which, in the form of the sanctified Gifts, the Lord of Glory Himself is present, the very Lord of Hosts! How does this poor and weak sinner dare to be so bold? How does the heavenly lightning, the heavenly fire, not burn and incinerate him to utter ashes? Trembling because of his weakness and in dread before his service, the priest raises his hands in crosswise fashion, as if to say, "Not I, Lord, no, not through my unclean hands but through Thy Cross I lift these Gifts up to Thee. I cover myself with the cross, I hope on the cross, and through it I offer this dread Divine service." The sign of the cross holds back the heavenly fire. This sign of the cross sanctifies the priest from every impurity and passion. And so, covered under the cross, he fearlessly stands before the face of the Lord, before Whom even the Seraphim cover themselves with their wings.

This sign of the cross has yet another meaning too. On behalf of all are the Gifts elevated, for all sins. But how, may we ask, for the forgiveness of our sins, how have we deserved such mercy? Moreover, since we at every step forget the commandments? Since we at every minute serve our own selves and our passions? How may we hope for forgiveness? Yes! We may hope, hope to receive forgiveness and the Mercy of God because the Sacrifice for our sins is raised up on the Cross. He covers all—all our lawlessness; this covering extends over the whole sinful world—erring, adulterous, and lying in evil. Lord, we are not worthy of Thy mercy! We are full of every impurity but we have the sufferings on the Cross of Thy Christ, and we show them to Thee, through these wounds we are covered, we beseech Thee, in the name of the Blood of Thy Son, forgive us all! This is what the crosswise holding of the priest's hands proclaims and this is why we dare boldly to hope for forgiveness. We receive this very forgiveness in the Divine Liturgy! It is the axis of the world. As a wheel may only spin

Homily 21: The Elevation of the Holy Gifts

when mounted on its axis, so our world, our wheel of life, is able to move only because the Divine Liturgy is served, for in the time of its service the Bloodless Sacrifice is raised on high. Let those who have no desire to gaze through the window of the Divine Liturgy be not exalted, for they trample underfoot the priceless pearl. I say, let no one imagine that he can truly live without the Divine Liturgy.

If people are alive, if they eat bread, if springs give forth water, if the sun shines on everyone, and the moon traverses the sky, then it is only because the Divine Liturgy is served; if it were not served, fire from heaven would have fallen on our heads long ago due to our lawlessness. Long ago we would have rotted away from our falls into the passions and we would have suffocated in the abyss of worldly cares.

The Cross is our anchor. The Cross is our covering; the virtues of the Cross are commemorated everyday at the Divine Liturgy. Only the Cross will save the world from final destruction. "The Cross is our protection."

HOMILY 22

The Consecration of the Holy Gifts

If a traveler in a scorching desert found a spring of water to quench his torturous thirst, about what do you think he would talk? Or if a person found a priceless pearl, of what do you think he would speak? Or if a sick person received healing from a deadly illness, about what do you think he would talk? The traveler will speak of the spring of water that quenched his thirst; the person who found the treasure will not cease to speak of what he has acquired; the healed person will praise the one who gave him the wondrous medicine. And so, having received the unspeakable mercy of God in the Divine Liturgy, of what can I speak but of this holy, mystical, great, and splendid Liturgy?

Today I will say a little bit about the fourth portion of the Eucharistic canon—the consecration of the Holy Gifts. But I will only say a little bit because there is so much one could say, even the entire life of a person would not provide enough time to touch on it all. Even more so, it is impossible for our impoverished and weak tongues to speak of that which for the angels is a subject of amazement.

Homily 22: The Consecration of the Holy Gifts

The Seraphim contemplate it with trembling awe, and it is beyond the full understanding of the Cherubim. Such is the dread mystery of the transformation of the Holy Gifts, that is the change of the bread and wine into the Holy and Most Pure Body and Blood of Christ Himself.

It should be noted that the Catholics do not count a fourth portion in their Eucharistic canon. They consider that at the moment when the words "*Take, eat*" are pronounced, on the altar is the Body of Christ. Our Orthodox Church holds that the transformation of the Holy Gifts happens at the time when the priest says the words "*And make this bread...*" and the other holy words. This is the substance of the fourth portion of the Eucharistic canon.

The priest having lifted the Gifts on high and exclaimed, "*Thine own of Thine own,*" then prays the sacred prayer, "*Again we offer unto Thee this rational and bloodless worship...*" as the choir sings "*We praise Thee....*"

What remarkable words are said! "*We supplicate Thee,*"[125] that is, we make ourselves beloved[126] of the Lord, His close ones, His dear ones. Such is the boundless and great mercy[127] of God. He allows us to count ourselves His beloved. Then the priest prays three times "*O Lord, Who didst send down Thy Most Holy Spirit....*"[128] He then makes the sign of the cross over the bread while saying, "*And make

---

125 In Slavonic, *И мили ся деем*

126 In Russian, *Милый*

127 In Russian, *Милосердие*. In the Russian there is a use of words that is difficult to convey in English, the words noted in the previous two footnotes and this one all share a common root in Russian. Thus, in the Russian/Slavonic word translated as "supplicate" is contained the understanding of being beloved and receiving mercy. For to have the ability to truly supplicate means that such are ones who are beloved and dear. The Lord will hearken unto those who are dear to Him.

128 This prayer is not used in Greek practice.

this bread..." and then signing the wine, he says, "*And that which is in this Cup...*" after which he blesses both the *diskos* and the cup, proclaiming, "*Making the change by Thy Holy Spirit. Amen. Amen. Amen.*" The pronouncement of these prayers indicates the very moment of the awesome transformation. From this moment, according to the teaching of the Church, on the altar is no longer bread and wine but the very Most Pure Body of Christ and the very Most Pure Blood of Christ. The priest then prostrates himself before the Holy Things.

With what trembling awe, with what reverence, must we stand at this moment before the face of God Himself. Think only of this, my dear ones! Because it is not one of the saints nor an angel of God, but the very Lord Himself Who is set before us, and before Him we offer our prayers. Before this miracle the Seraphim stand with awe and the Cherubim look on Him with amazement; the host of heavenly powers descends to the altar so to have only a glimpse of this gift, which mankind has received according to the unspeakable love of God.

This moment of the Divine Liturgy is the very foundation of all life on earth, it is the axis upon which the wheel of life turns. As a wheel cannot effectively move and will eventually fall over without an axis, so it is with our world—passion filled, sinful, all rotten from impurity and lawlessness; it would perish, disintegrate, and be destroyed if the great, mystical, and dread revelation of the Divine Redeemer was not consecrated in the temple on the altar. In that moment[129] the altar is sanctified, and the temple, and the worshippers, and the grounds around the church, and all the homes of this parish and those living in them together with all their belongings, labors, and the fruit of their labors; the earth is sanctified and gives bread and wine for the Divine Sacrifice, and even the very air is sanc-

---

129 I.e., the moment of the consecration of the Holy Gifts

tified. Nature serves a person and gives what is needed for living only because for him the Holy Lamb, our Lord Jesus Christ, is present on the *diskos* and in the chalice under the form of bread and wine.

How fearful is this moment—the whole existence of a person, all his feelings, thoughts, and all his being must prostrate before this manifestation of the Redeemer's love and mercy for mankind. And our sinful and lawless world will continue to exist, and the earth will bring forth harvests of food for both people and animals, and the sun, moon, and stars will give light as long as the Divine Liturgy is offered on the face of the earth. But when, with the coming of the Antichrist, believers will be forced to go underground—there to offer the Divine Liturgy, there to lift up the Bloodless Sacrifice—at that time our world will perish; the heavenly lights will fade and fall, the springs of water will dry up, the the earth will wither and cease giving forth its fruit. Then that terrible time will come of which it is said that people will cry out for the mountains and hills to "fall on them."[130] But as long as the Most Pure Body is present in the temple, as long as people worship Him, let us not fear any woe or any adversity of this life. Death is not fearful because gazing on Jesus Christ present (on the altar) we may boldly hope for deliverance. The Lord, Who gives His very Self cannot but hear us when we cry to Him at the moment of His manifestation on the Holy Altar.

---

130 cf. Rev. 6:16

Saint Seraphim Zvezdinsky

A Prayer to the New Hieromartyr Seraphim

O glorious God-pleaser, Hieromartyr Seraphim, a quick helper and intercessor on our behalf, with faith we run to thee! Having loved Christ from thy youth and following the monastic path, thou art revealed as a good shepherd. In the days of severe persecution against the Church in Russia, thou didst fearlessly take up the *podvig* of confession, while enduring persecution and suffering, and sealing thy faithfulness to Christ with thy blood, thereby receiving a martyr's crown. Therefore, we bend the knee of our hearts, as thy faithful children, and pray thee, strengthen us in love for the Lord so that we may stand steadfastly for the Orthodox Faith; guard us from schisms and false teachings; grant to our homeland peace and godliness. Help us, O confessor of Christ, to pass the time of our life on earth in virtue, righteousness, and godliness. Cover us with thy heavenly blessings and pray to the Lord on our behalf, that through thine intercessions and protection it will be given unto us to enter into the Kingdom of Heaven, where together with thee we may glorify God Who is wondrous in His saints, the Trinity, magnifying the Father, and the Son, and the Holy Spirit, unto the ages of ages. Amen.

Bishop Seraphim Zvezdinsky in Ishi, the place of his martyrdom.

The Theotokos Prayer Rule

The Theotokos Prayer Rule has been greatly encouraged, in relatively recent times, by both Ss. Seraphim (Zvezdinsky) and Seraphim of Sarov. There are also a number of other righteous ones, mostly from Russia (pre-revolutionary), who deeply encourage the practice of this rule in some form, there are a few forms as to which the believer may strive to undertake. These righteous ones testify that the Theotokos Rule originated in the eight century.

The central form of this prayer rule consists of praying, "*O Theotokos and Virgin, rejoice, Mary, full of grace, the Lord is with thee; blessed art thou among women, and blessed is the Fruit of thy womb, for thou hast borne the Savior of our souls,*" one hundred and fifty times. This is the rule as given by St. Seraphim of Sarov.

Typically this prayer is done in "decades," that is, sets of ten. After each decade, the "*Our Father*" is recited once together with the prayer, "*The door of compassion open unto us, O blessed Theotokos, for, hoping in thee may we not perish; through thee may we be delivered from adversities, for thou art the salvation of the Christian race.*"

The last saintly Elder of St. Sergius Lavra, who suffered greatly under Soviet oppression and persecution, Zachariah (his name before his tonsure into the great-schema was Zosima) also fervently encouraged the practice of the Theotokos Rule. "When the elder turned to the Heavenly Queen in prayer, he spoke to her as though she were alive and he could see her right there in his cell. And in fact, the Heavenly Queen was always with him, and the entire inner and outward life of the elder passed under her protection. And he exhorted all his spiritual children to say daily, every hour of the twenty-four, 'O Theotokos and Virgin, Rejoice,' (the whole prayer to the end) and to beg for the blessing of the Ever Virgin Mary on every hour of their lives and on the lives of those near them.

The elder rejoiced if any of his spiritual children fulfilled the Theotokos Prayer Rule, saying *"O Theotokos and Virgin, Rejoice ..."* one hundred and fifty times a day.

The Heavenly Queen herself had given this Rule. However, everyone had forgotten it. They had forgotten about obedience to Our Lady Who Shows the Way [Directress], the Joy Above All Joys.

St. Seraphim [of Sarov] had reminded people of this Rule, making them walk along the ditch that encircled the Convent of Diveevo saying the prayer "O Theotokos and Virgin, Rejoice" one hundred and fifty times. He instructed his spiritual children to fulfill this rule."[131]

A very respected hieromonk, Fr. Alexander Gumanovsky, also greatly encouraged the practice of the Theotokos Rule. He is mentioned briefly in an exhaustive collection of the lives of the New Martyrs of Russia, *"One old priest monk, Fr. Alexander Gumanovsky, selflessly travelled everywhere that he was called, and the Lord even managed that he should give communion to the sick in hospitals. Sitting by them like a visitor, he confessed them and then, as if giving them some medicine or food, gave them Holy Communion."*[132]

---

131 Ellis, Jane. *An Early Soviet Saint, the Life of Father Zachariah, by One of His Spiritual Daughters.* Templegate Publishers, 1976. Pg. 66-65.

132 https://dnjosephsuaiden.typepad.com/blog/2009/04/the-life-

Another source records this account of the hieromonk, "Father Alexander Gumanovsky (whose monastic name was Daniel), was gentle and quiet, completely buried in his love for the Heavenly Queen. His whole life was constant servitude to the Ever Virgin Mary; all his spiritual children repeated one hundred and fifty prayers daily to the Mother of God, and some of them had been favored with a passage into eternal life, offering up the good news of the Archangel to her who is more honorable than the cherubim and more glorious beyond compare than the seraphim.

Here is an extract from a letter of that most gentle man, Father Alexander Gumanovsky, who because of his love for the Heavenly Queen was nicknamed 'the Mother of God's' elder by one of his spiritual children.

'... I forgot to give you a piece of advice vital for salvation. Say the 'O Theotokos and Virgin, Rejoice' one hundred and fifty times, and this prayer will save you. This Rule was given by the Mother of God herself in about the eighth century, and at one time all Christians fulfilled it. We Orthodox have forgotten about it, and St. Seraphim has reminded us of this Rule. In my own hands I have a handwritten book from the cell of St. Seraphim, containing a description of the many miracles which took place through saying one hundred and fifty repetitions daily, 'O Theotokos and Virgin, Rejoice.' If being unaccustomed to it, it is difficult to master one hundred and fifty repetitions daily, say it fifty times at first. After every ten repetitions say the 'Our Father' once and 'The doors of compassion open unto us.' Whoever he spoke to about this miracle-working Rule remained grateful to him.'"[133]

---

of-hieromartyr-joseph-metropolitan-of-petrograd-and-those-with-him.html Accessed on January 10, 2024.

[133] Ellis, Jane. *An Early Soviet Saint, the Life of Father Zachariah, by One of His Spiritual Daughters.* Templegate Publishers, 1976. Pg. 66-67.

The extended prayers, provided below, as given by St. Seraphim Zvezdinsky seem to be his own unique additions to this Prayer Rule. Elder Zachariah states that this extended Prayer Rule is difficult for most people to fulfill. Those who desire to begin the practice of the Theotokos Prayer Rule should follow the method as given above by St. Seraphim of Sarov. Even then, it may be needed to ease into it by starting with a rule of fifty times a day. As with any addition to a person's existing general prayer rule, the believer should check with his spiritual father before taking on any extra prayers.

The extended prayer rule as given by St. Seraphim Zvezdinsky[134]

These additional prayers may be prayed after each decade. This rule was fulfilled by the Hieromartyr Seraphim (Zvezdinsky) and in doing so he prayed for the whole world while embracing the entire life of the Heavenly Queen:

THE FIRST DECADE:
We remember the Nativity of the Blessed Virgin Mary. Here we offer prays for mothers, fathers and children.
"O Most Holy Lady Theotokos, save and protect thy servants (names of parents and relatives), and to the departed grant rest with the saints in thine eternal glory."

THE SECOND DECADE:
We remember the Entry into the Temple of the Blessed Virgin Mary. Here we pray for those who have gone astray and fallen away from the Church.
"O, Most holy Lady Theotokos, save and protect and reunite (or join) to the Holy Orthodox Church thy lost and fallen away servants (names)."

---

134 See publisher's note on page 116.

The Theotokos Prayer Rule

THE THIRD DECADE:

We remember the Annunciation of the Most Holy Theotokos. Here we pray for the soothing of sorrows and consolation of those who mourn.

"O, Most Holy Lady Theotokos, soothe our sorrows and send consolation to thy servants (names) who are grieving or sick."

THE FOURTH DECADE:

We remember the Meeting of the Most Holy Theotokos with Righteous Elizabeth. Here we pray for the reunion of those who have been estranged and those missing or separated from relatives or children.

"O, Most Holy Lady Theotokos, unite Thy servants (names) who have been separated."

THE FIFTH DECADE:

We remember the Nativity of Christ and we pray for the rebirth of souls and for the new life that is in Christ.

"O, Most Holy Lady Theotokos, grant me, who was baptized into Christ, to put on Christ."

THE SIXTH DECADE:

We remember the Meeting of the Lord and the word prophesied by St. Symeon: "And a sword will pierce thy soul." Here we pray that the Mother of God would meet our soul at the hour of death and that we would be worthy, with our last breath, to partake of the Holy Mysteries and that She would lead the soul through the terrible ordeals [toll-houses].

"O, Most Holy Lady Theotokos, grant me with my last breath to partake of the Holy Mysteries of Christ and do thou thyself lead my soul through the terrible ordeals [of the toll-houses]."

THE SEVENTH DECADE:

We remember the flight of the Mother of God with the Divine Infant to Egypt. Here we pray that the Heavenly Queen would help us to avoid temptations in this life and save us from misfortunes.

"O, Most Holy Lady Theotokos, let me not be led into temptation in this life and deliver me from all misfortunes."

THE EIGHTH DECADE:

We remember how the twelve year-old Jesus was seemingly lost during a trip to Jerusalem and how the Mother of God grieved over this. Here we pray, asking the Mother of God for the constant praying of the Jesus Prayer.

"O, Most Holy Lady Theotokos, Most Pure Virgin Mary, grant me to pray unceasingly the Jesus Prayer."

THE NINTH DECADE:

We remember the miracle in Cana of Galilee, when the Lord turned water into wine according to the word of the Mother of God: "They have no wine." Here we ask the Mother of God for help in our undertakings and for deliverance from need.

"O, Most Holy Lady Theotokos, help me in every enterprise and deliver me from all needs and sorrows."

THE TENTH DECADE:

We remember how the Mother of God stood at the Cross of the Lord and sorrow, like a sword, pierced her soul. Here we pray to the Most-Pure One for the strengthening of our spiritual fortitude and for the driving away of despondency.

"O, Most Holy Lady Theotokos, Blessed Virgin Mary, strengthen my spiritual fortitude and drive despondency far from me."

The Theotokos Prayer Rule

THE ELEVENTH DECADE:

We remember the Resurrection of Christ and prayerfully ask the Mother of God to resurrect our soul and give new vigor to our spiritual contest [*podvig*].

"O, Most Holy Lady Theotokos, resurrect my soul and grant me constant readiness for spiritual contest [podvig]."

THE TWELFTH DECADE:

We remember the Ascension of Christ, at which the Mother of God was present. Here we pray and ask the Heavenly Queen to raise the soul above earthly and vain amusements and direct it towards striving for heavenly things.

"O, Most Holy Lady Theotokos, deliver me from vain thoughts and grant me a mind and a heart that strives for the salvation of the soul."

THE THIRTEENTH DECADE:

We remember the upper chamber at Zion and the descent of the Holy Spirit on the apostles and the Mother of God while praying: "Create a pure heart in me, O God, and renew a right spirit within me. Cast me not away from Thy presence, and take not Thy Holy Spirit from me."

"O, Most Holy Lady Theotokos, send down into my heart and strengthen within it the grace of the Holy Spirit."

THE FOURTEENTH DECADE:

We remember the Dormition of the Most Holy Theotokos and ask for a peaceful and serene death.

"O, Most Holy Lady Theotokos, grant me a peaceful and serene ending to my life."

THE FIFTEENTH DECADE:

We remember the glory of the Mother of God, with which She is crowned by the Lord after She was taken from earth to Heaven, and we pray the Heavenly Queen not to forsake the faithful who are on earth, but to protect them from all evil, covering them with Her Most-Honorable *Omophor* [Protection].

"O, Most Holy Lady Theotokos, save me from all evil and cover me with thy Most-Honorable Omophor [Protection]."

Publisher's Note:

As stated, these added prayers at the end of each decade are uniquely attributed to St. Seraphim (Zvezdinsky) and are not commonly found in writings of other Orthodox saints. Some may ask how this particular prayer rule differs from the Latin use of the Rosary. The prayer, "O Theotokos and Virgin, rejoice..." was used widely in the East and West before the Great Schism. Prayer ropes and beads were also used from the earliest centuries of the Church, though in the Orthodox Church the prayer rope is most commonly used for the Jesus Prayer, "Lord Jesus Christ have mercy on me" as well as the prayer to the Theotokos, "Most Holy Theotokos, save us!" In the West after the Great Schism, "mysteries" were introduced to praying of the Rosary by Dominic of Prussia in the 15th century for reflection on specific events in the lives of the Lord Jesus Christ and the Theotokos. Also, after the Schism, the imagination was increasingly utilized in prayer in the West despite being strictly forbidden by the saints and Fathers before the Schism (and Orthodox saints after the Schism) as leading to spiritual deception and delusion. In the West, Ignatius of Loyola who founded the Jesuits in the 16th century, advocated the use of the imagination in prayer and in the reading of the Scriptures. Such an approach often includes instructions to "Visualize the event as if you were making a movie. Pay attention to the details: sights, sounds, tastes, smells, and feelings of the event. Lose yourself in the story; don't worry if your imagination is running too wild. At some point, place yourself in the scene."[135] Since the 16th century, this imaginative approach increasingly began to characterize prayer in the West. By contrast, the great 19th century Russian Saint Ignatius (Brianchaninov) expresses the Orthodox and patristic approach to prayer when he says, "The most dangerous of the incorrect types of prayer consists of the person creating imaginary pictures, seemingly borrowing them from the Holy Scripture, but in reality—from his own state of fall and self-pride; and with these pictures he flatters his own self-opinion, his fall, his sinfulness, deceives himself. Obviously, everything which is created by the imagination of our fallen nature, does not exist in reality, is make-belief and false... The one who imagines, with the first step on the path of prayer leaves the area of truth and enters the area of deceit, passions, sin, Satan." (St. Ignatius Brianchaninov, *Collected works. 6 vols, The Rule of Faith*: Moscow, 2004. 1:160-1, in Russian). Among the Orthodox saints from ancient times to the present, it is common to find instructions to reflect on one's sins, on death, on the Final Judgment, and other themes as a way to cultivate contrition of heart and pray more deeply, but such reflection is encouraged to be done briefly and without stirring up the imagination. With this in mind, the "reflections" proposed by St. Seraphim (Svezdinsky) are not problematic for Orthodox if approached in a sober way, not giving in to imagination and fantasy in the Latin and Ignatian manner.

---

135 See Kevin O'Brien, SJ, "Ignatian Contemplation: Imaginative Prayer," Ignatian Spirituality, accessed January 15, 2024. https://www.ignatianspirituality.com/ignatian-prayer/the-spiritual-exercises/ignatian-contemplation-imaginative-prayer/

Hieromartyr Seraphim Zvezdinsky, Bishop of Dmitrovsky

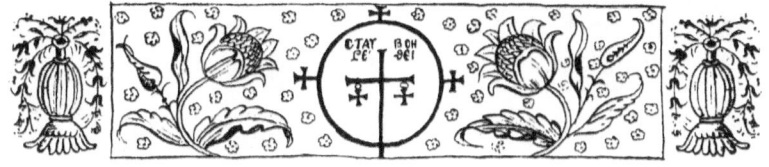

BIOGRAPHY OF ST. SERAPHIM ZVEZDINSKY

Commemorated on the Sunday nearest the 25th of January

The New Martyrs of Russia

The Holy Hieromartyr Seraphim was born on April 7th, 1883, with the name Nikolai Ivanovich Zvezdinsky. His pious family belonged to the "Edinoverets" Church, a canonical Old Believer community. His father was a priest, and they had a special veneration for the elder Seraphim of Sarov, who, at that time, had yet to be formally glorified. The prayers and holy protection of the elder surrounded the young Nikolai throughout his life, especially in the miraculous healing of an incurable illness as he stood at vigil before his icon. A year later, he stood amidst the throngs of faithful and the Imperial Family as they celebrated the solemn glorification of his heavenly intercessor, St. Seraphim of Sarov.

Upon graduating from the Moscow Theological Academy, Nikolai was later tonsured a monk with the name Seraphim in honor of his patron. Thus began his life in total service to the Holy Orthodox Church and the beginning of his path of martyrdom for Christ.

St. Seraphim was Abbot of the Chudov Monastery inside Moscow's Kremlin amidst the demonic terror of the October Revolution, an event after which the representatives of the self-appointed authorities ordered the monastery to begin ousting the struggling monks. By July, Bishop Arseniy (Zhadanovsky) and then-Archimandrite Seraphim fled to the wilderness, eventually finding refuge at a cell prepared by a spiritual daughter of the bishop near the Znamensky skete. It was there that the Saint continued his ascetic life—praying the daily services, tending garden beds, and chopping wood—and it was from there he was called back to Moscow for ordination to the bishopric by His Holiness, Patriarch (Saint) Tikhon.

The few years St. Seraphim served as shepherd to the flock of the city of Dimitrov would leave an indelible impression on their hearts. Large crowds often awaited him at the end of Divine Services, where they would envelop his carriage chanting Akathists and prayers as they escorted him back to his residence. However, the heroic contests of the noble athlete of the Lord did not go unnoticed by the evil one, and the hostile *Bogobortsi* (God-fighters) of the soviet regime attacked him relentlessly with slanderous propaganda in a vain attempt to discredit the work of the Holy Hieromartyr. In return for his labors, the secret police repaid him with constant surveillance and arrested him six times over the following decade.

After numerous struggles, accusations of "counter-revolutionary activity", forced exile, and illness, St. Seraphim was arrested a final time on June 24th, 1937. In one of his final letters, he wrote: "I feel serene, cheerful and upbeat. The Lord gives me strength and inspires me to feel right about my stand, despite grave circumstances." On the

26th of August, 1937, the NKVD (Soviet Secret Police) executed St. Seraphim by firing squad in the city of Omsk.

The Saint of God possessed the gifts of clairvoyance, prayer, and healing the sick in a time of apostasy coupled with subversion, crime joined with madness, showing forth the truth of the words of the Lord: "I am with you, even to the end of the age."

He was glorified among the New Martyrs of Russia in the year 2000.

St. Seraphim Zvezdinksy, pray to God for us!

Hieromartyr Seraphim (Zvezdinsky),
Bishop of Dmitrovsky

UNCUT MOUNTAIN PRESS TITLES

Books by Archpriest Peter Heers

Fr. Peter Heers, *The Ecclesiological Renovation of Vatican II: An Orthodox Examination of Rome's Ecumenical Theology Regarding Baptism and the Church*, 2015

Fr. Peter Heers, *The Missionary Origins of Modern Ecumenism: Milestones Leading up to 1920*, 2007

The Works of our Father Among the Saints, Nikodemos the Hagiorite

Vol. 1: *Exomologetarion: A Manual of Confession*
Vol. 2: *Concerning Frequent Communion of the Immaculate Mysteries of Christ*
Vol. 3: *Confession of Faith*

Other Available Titles

Elder Cleopa of Romania, *The Truth of our Faith*
Elder Cleopa of Romania, *The Truth of our Faith, Vol. II*
Fr. John Romanides, *Patristic Theology: The University Lectures of Fr. John Romanides*
Demetrios Aslanidis and Monk Damascene Grigoriatis, *Apostle to Zaire: The Life and Legacy of Blessed Father Cosmas of Grigoriou*
Protopresbyter Anastasios Gotsopoulos, *On Common Prayer with the Heterodox According to the Canons of the Church*
Robert Spencer, *The Church and the Pope*
G. M. Davis, *Antichrist: The Fulfillment of Globalization*
Athonite Fathers of the 20th Century, Vol. I
St. Gregory Palamas, *Apodictic Treatises on the Procession of the Holy Spirit*
St. Hilarion (Troitsky), *On the Dogma of the Church: An Historical Overview of the Sources of Ecclesiology*
Fr. Alexander Webster and Fr. Peter Heers, Editors, *Let No One Fear Death*
Subdeacon Nektarios Harrison, *Metropolitan Philaret of New York*
Elder George of Grigoriou, *Catholicism in the Light of Orthodoxy*
Archimandrite Ephraim Triandaphillopoulos, *Noetic Prayer as the Basis of Mission and the Struggle Against Heresy*
Dr. Nicholas Baldimtsis, *Life and Witness of St. Iakovos of Evia*
On the Reception of the Heterodox into the Orthodox Church: The Patristic Consensus and Criteria
Patrick (Craig) Truglia, *The Rise and Fall of the Papacy*
St. Raphael of Brooklyn, *In Defense of St. Cyprian*

The Divine Service of the Eighth Œcumenical Council
The Orthodox Patristic Witness Concerning Catholicism

Select Forthcoming Titles

Cell of the Resurrection, Mount Athos, *On the Mystery of Christ: An Athonite Catechism*
Minutes of the Eighth Œcumenical Council
Georgio (Pachymeres), *Errors of the Latins*
Fr. George Metallinos, *I Confess One Baptism*, 2nd Edition
St. Maximus the Confessor, *Opuscula: Theological and Polemical Works*
Fr. Peter Heers, *Going Deeper in the Spiritual Life*
Fr. Peter Heers, *On the Body of Christ and Baptism*
Athonite Fathers of the 20th Century, Vol. II

This 1ˢᵗ Edition of
Homilies on the Divine Liturgy
written by Hieromartyr Seraphim Zvezdinsky, translated by Father Zechariah Lynch, typeset in Baskerville in this two thousand and twenty fourth year of our Lord's Holy Incarnation is one of the many fine titles available from Uncut Mountain Press, translators and publishers of Orthodox Christian theological and spiritual literature. Find the book you are looking for at

u n c u t m o u n t a i n p r e s s . c o m

**GLORY BE TO GOD
FOR ALL THINGS**

AMEN.

www.ingramcontent.com/pod-product-compliance
Lightning Source LLC
Chambersburg PA
CBHW030556080526
44585CB00012B/388